PARADISE
LOST

THE
NOVEL

PARADISE LOST

The Novel

Based upon the
Epic Poem by

JOHN MILTON

by Joseph Lanzara

New
ARTS
Library

ISBN 0-9639621-4-0 hardcover
ISBN 0-9639621-3-2 paperback
ISBN 978-0-9639621-3-3 paperback
Library of Congress Control Number: 2008934510

Cover design by Joseph Lanzara

Published by New Arts Library
P.O. Box 319, Belleville, New Jersey 07109

Printed in the United States of America

www.paradiselost.org

Contents:

1

Revolt in Heaven

THE FALL of man came at noon in Eden, where mortal taste of forbidden fruit brought death into the world, and all our woe. What cause led our great parents, in their happy state, favored so highly by Heaven, to fall away from their Creator and transgress his will? Who first seduced them to that foul revolt, and how, and why?

High matters to pursue. For how may earthly language impart things above earthly thought, which yet concern our knowing?—things as strange and unimaginable as hate in Heaven and violence in the kingdom of God. A sad and difficult task it is, to tell of warring angels and the ruin of so many, once glorious and perfect while they stood. How shall these pages relate to human sense the secrets of another world?—things yet unattempted in prose or poem, perhaps unlawful to reveal to man, created

1

without faculty to understand his own creation. Is the proportion of heavenly events unmeasurable by planetary scale, or do the ways of gods, perhaps after all, parallel those of men? What if Earth is but the shadow of Heaven, and things in each much like the other, more so than on Earth is thought?

Envision, then, these invisible exploits through words that liken spiritual to human forms, and paint in earthly hue realms divine, as may to earthly thought express them best. Look first beyond these heavens we view so high, to that time when they rolled yet unadorned with stars, when this world as yet did not exist and Chaos reigned where Earth now spins, and behold a host of innumerable multitudes of angels called together from all the ends of Heaven by imperial summons before the Almighty's throne.

The day is one of great mystical high celebration, a day borne of Heaven's eternal year, before human time has yet begun it's count. Thousands upon thousands in order of receding rank they stand, in concentric waves radiating from the holy mount. Orb within orb, in reverent anticipation they circle the Infinite Father. From front to rear, high waving ensigns and glittering banners commemorating holy acts of zeal and love stream in the air and serve to distinguish the various bright orders and degrees of hierarchies: thrones, dominations, princedoms, virtues, powers, and brightest seraphim. They approach not the inaccessible throne upon the flaming mount, whose top is rendered invisible by brightness, but with both wings veil their eyes. For no creature, whether flesh or spirit, can behold the full blaze of his beams that dazzle Heaven with a fountain of light. But when all have assembled, the Eternal Father draws round him misty shade, and through a golden cloud his robed image becomes visible as a radiant shrine, beside which, in equal brilliance, appears the begotten Son, his divine counterpart in love consummate. In the Son's countenance the glory of the Almighty shines, newly reflected, his spirit transfused.

From his eternal seat the Lord High Father speaks:

"Hear all ye angels, children of light, hear my decree, which henceforth shall stand: This day, on this holy hill, I have anointed my only begotten Son, that he may reign over you at my right hand. Before him all knees in Heaven shall bend, and under his appointed power shall you abide, united as one undivided soul, forever happy. He who disobeys my Son, disobeys me, and shall that day be cast out from my sight into utter darkness forever."

Universal accord met his holy dictum, or so then it seemed, and that day was spent as other solemn days of Heaven, in song and dance about the sacred hill. Involved mazes and wheels compounded the mystical dances of those immortal angels. Yet, as in the intricate motions of stars and planets, when most involved they seemed, order appeared and divine harmony. Of such charm was their music even God's ear was delighted. As evening approached, tables were piled with fruits from Heaven's delicious vines. Ruby nectar flowed in goblets of pearl and diamond. The angels reposed upon seats of flowers, crowns of stringed flowerets upon their heads, and they ate and drank of the abundance laid before them by the generous hand of their benign King, who rejoiced in their pleasure. When night came, it was in the color of twilight, for night comes not there in darker veil, where it falls not by necessity, but for pleasing variety. The dew of roses made heavy all but the unsleeping eye of God, and wide over all the plain, wider far than all the plains of Earth combined, the angelic throng spread out in bands and made camp along living streams and among the trees of life, within new raised shelters of numberless pavilions and tabernacles, as all night long the cool winds carried melodious hymns to the sovereign throne.

But it was not those mellow sounds that kept awake one whose name is heard in Heaven no more. One great in power and held in great favor—highest of the archangels—was now fraught with envy against the Son of God. As the midnight hour drew on, the restless angel awakened his next subordinate, who lay beside him:

"Comrade, what sleep can close your eyelids, having heard from the lips of Heaven's imperious Ruler that oppressive decree whose echo cancels all chance of peace this night? Your eyes spoke volumes to me then; now, drooping, they yield to proffered wine and placating night songs. Shall we then mindlessly submit to new laws imposed by him who newly reigns, or first debate what this may mean?"

But he stayed his companion's reply with a gesture, for such exchange was unsafe so near the ear of God. Pride, first deadly influence, had invaded the archangel and infused in his breast fear, envy, and bad thoughts that this day's honoring of the Son of God—proclaimed Anointed King by his Great Father—had somehow left him the less. He

gave orders for all who carried his banner to be
assembled before night withdrew and proceed in
flying march to their quarters in the north:

"Soon our youthful king shall pass triumphantly
through all the hierarchies, giving laws. Let us pre-
pare a fitting reception to the Great Messiah and
his new commands."

The conspiring companion quickly rose and in
secret called up separately each of the regent powers
under his leader's command. He conveyed the
orders to move, while casting suggestions between
ambiguous words aimed to taint integrity and sound
out their loyalty, one by one. But all unquestioningly
obeyed the signal handed down from their great
potentate, who drew with him fully one-third of
Heaven's host. God's eye, whose sight discerns all
Heaven's most hidden thoughts, saw the rebellion
rising and knew already how many and which
multitudes were banding to oppose his decree.
Across the golden lamps that nightly burn within his
high abode, he spoke to his only heir:

"Son of all my glory, behold, an enemy is rising
who intends to erect his throne equal to ours
throughout the sacred north, and not content with
this, is thinking to test our power in battle. Let us
make plans and quickly draw what forces we have
left to our defense, to hold what anciently we claim,
our sanctuary and our empire."

"Almighty Father," the Son responded, "their vain
and foolish revolt can only serve to make greater my
own glory, when they witness the power you shall
give me to crush their uprising."

Meanwhile, on winged speed, the rebel angel and
his powers, innumerable as the stars of night, passed

over regions greater than all the dominions of earth and sea, at length coming to the limits of the north. They assembled at his royal seat high on a hill, a mountain raised upon a mountain, with pyramids and towers hewn from diamond quarries and rocks of gold, built in imitation of the holy mount, in vain aspiration to equality with God.

The palace of Lucifer, Son of Light.

Here he held the ears of the congregation, practicing his unholy skills of slanderous persuasion:

"Thrones, dominations, princedoms, virtues, powers—(if these, your magnificent orders, still hold as more than empty titles, now eclipsed by another, who by decree claims all power under his new title of Anointed King)—the purpose of your midnight march to this hurried meeting is to consult how best we may honor and pay tribute to him when he shall come to extend his golden scepter over us, requiring bows and prostrate worship, already given too much to one, now to be doubly endured for Father and Son alike.

"A new yoke is dangled before you; will you happily kneel and submit your necks? Not happily, if I know you as I think I do, or if you know yourselves, native sons of Heaven, never before owned by anyone—perhaps not all equal, but all equally free. Your orders and degrees have never impeded your liberty, but have worked in harmony with it. In reason, who then can assume monarchy over such as we who live rightfully as his peers, if less than him in power and splendor, at least equal in freedom? Shall he now impart law and edict on us, who without law have lived long and well and without error? Moreover, the task is transferred to secondary hands: our sudden appointed Lord, the favored offspring, who seeks adoration from us, rendering meaningless those imperial titles which assert that we be ordained to govern and not to serve."

From among the audience suddenly up stood the seraph, Abdiel, to oppose the current of Lucifer's malice. None adored the Deity or obeyed his divine commands with more zeal than he who passionately now spoke:

"No ear in Heaven has expected ever to hear an argument so proud, false, and profane—from you, least of all, who are placed so high above your peers by him you now deride. Ingrate! How dare you condemn the just decree of God with your abusive words! Will you dispute the points of liberty with him that formed the very powers of Heaven and made you what you are? We should all well know by experience how good and prudent he is in his concern for our welfare and our dignity. How far from his mind is the thought to make less of us, but rather to heighten and intensify our happy state by letting all be more closely united under one head.

"The Mighty Father made all things—even you— and all the spirits of Heaven. He created them in their bright degrees and crowned them with glory. Nor are they obscured by his reign, but made more illustrious. With him as our head our number reduces to one, his laws become our laws, and all honor done to him returns again to us. Cease then your impious questions, and do not tempt these spirits! Hasten to withdraw your impetuous words before they have gone too far!"

Paradise Lost

Fervently the courageous angel spoke, but no one seconded Abdiel's sentiment, much to Lucifer's pleasure and encouragement. Such is the advantage of being in one's own court. Here, where the loyal and the rebellious were transposed, the subordinate angel was judged brash and out of place by those who had earlier lent their praise alongside his to another master. Now in a different and distant quarter, easily intimidated by the prevailing rule, agile minds did sway and succumb to artful agitation, and less-skillful thinkers drifted comfortably with the majority, till all were unified in blasphemous discontent, save one.

"Do I hear that we were 'formed'?" said Lucifer. "Strange point and new! We would all like to know where you learned this doctrine. Who saw this creation? Do you remember your own making? Did you watch as the Maker gave you being? As for us, we know of no time when we did not exist as now. We know of none who existed before us. We are self-conceived, self-raised by our own evolving power. Our strength is our own. Our own right hand shall teach us highest deeds to prove for all to know who is or is not our equal. Then shall you see if we intend to approach tyranny in duty and humility—whether we surround the Almighty Throne beseeching or besieging!"

Hoarse murmuring echoed approval of Lucifer's words throughout the infinite host. But no less bold was Abdiel's reply, encompassed though he was by foes:

"I see your inevitable fall, Lucifer, and that of all your hapless crew, infected by your treachery. Do not trouble yourselves over how to quit the yoke of

God's Messiah. Those gentle laws are not for you. Harsher decrees against you soon shall take their place. Await no golden scepter to meet your scorn, but an iron rod that will bruise and break your disobedience!"

"Enough!" Here Lucifer's patience ended. "Your overzealous tongue finds weak purpose here. Take it back to him that welcomes your pious mouthings. And fly speedily, while your flight remains unimpeded!"

"I shall go," answered Abdiel, "though it is not your threat I flee, but these doomed tents, for when his impending wrath rages into flame, none who abide with you shall be spared. Soon expect to feel his thunder upon your head. Then learn who created you, and how he who creates can uncreate as well!"

With this Abdiel made away from Lucifer's increasing wrath. Without fear he moved amid looks of hostile scorn, flinging them back into the faces from whence they came, at last turning his back forever on those proud towers doomed to swift destruction.

All night across the wide celestial plain he held his way unpursued, till the circling hours unbarred the gates of Heaven's light. Morning arrived arrayed in imperial gold as a blazing horizon thick with embattled squadrons met his view. Flaming chariots and fiery steeds reflected the first beams of daybreak. He perceived war in readiness—evidence the news he had come to report was already known. Gladly Abdiel mixed among those friendly powers, who received him with joy and loud acclamations, that of so many myriads fallen, yet one returned not lost. They led him high on to the sacred hill, and applauding, presented him before the Throne Supreme.

"Servant of God, well done," spoke the mild voice from the midst of a shining cloud. "Well have you fought alone against the revolted multitudes. In speaking the truth you have borne universal reproach, far worse than violence to bear. An easier conquest now remains for you. Aided by this host of friends, you shall return to subdue your foes, returning in glory where scorned you did depart."

The Almighty then ordered Michael, prince of celestial armies, and Gabriel, next in military rank, to lead the armed saints into battle:

"Assault them with fire and drive them to the brow of Heaven, out from peace and bliss, into their place of punishment, the gulf of Tartarus, whose fiery chaos opens wide, ready to receive their fall."

Clouds began to darken the hill and smoke rolled in dusky wreaths as the ethereal trumpet blew from on high, the signal of dreadful wrath awakened. At its command, the militant powers that stood for Heaven joined in mighty formation. By thousands and millions they formed, equal in number to the godless rebel crew. The bright legions under their godlike leaders moved on in swift silence, eager for adventure and heroic deeds in the cause of God and his Messiah. Indissolubly firm in their perfect ranks they moved, neither constrained by valley or wood, nor divided by stream, for high above the ground was their march, the passive air upbearer of their nimble tread. It was as if the total kind and number of birds on Earth at once took flight together in orderly array.

Revolt in Heaven

Over many a tract of Heaven they marched, and many a province wide, in length tenfold that of this starry universe. At last far to the north appeared a fiery region, warlike in aspect stretched along the endless horizon. In closer view, the land bristled with innumerable upright beams of rigid spears, a throng of helmets, and various shields boasting heraldic slogans. The banded powers of Lucifer were approaching with furious speed, for they had thought that selfsame day to win by surprise attack the mount of God. Now midway, their endeavor proved naive and vain.

How strange it seems for us to think of angels at war, those gentle sons of one Great Sire, more naturally thought of singing hymns to the Eternal Father, united in festivals of joy and love. Yet here, on this immense plain of Heaven, the dreadful shout of battle now began. Between armies only a narrow interval was left as they halted on the rough edge of war and stood front to front, in a terrible array of hideous length. High in the midst of his darkly foreboding vanguard, exalted as a god, sat the apostate, Lucifer, idol of divine majesty, in his sun-bright chariot, enclosed with flaming cherubim and golden shields. Amid deadly silence, he alighted from his gorgeous throne and with vast and haughty strides advanced.

That towering sight, seen from where he stood among the mightiest, Abdiel could not endure—that such resemblance of the Highest should yet remain where faith and honesty did not. Should not strength and might fail where virtue fails, and boldest prove weakest, though in appearance unconquerable? Trusting in the Almighty's aid, he stepped forth, meaning to try Lucifer's power, as had his reason been tried and found unsound. For was it not just, that he who had won in debate of truth should win in dispute of arms as well? If reason had to deal in force, though brutish and foul that contest, so let it be by force that reason overcome. Confidently Abdiel met his foe halfway, where Lucifer, all the more incensed at this delay, addressed him:

"You return from flight, seditious angel, to receive your merited reward, first test of this right hand provoked since first that tongue inspired with contradiction did oppose me. But it is well you come before your fellows, ambitious to win from me some trophy. Let your ill fortune show the rest what destruction to expect."

"You are met, Lucifer," the brave angel answered with quiet defiance, "for as you see, all are not of your following. There be those who prefer faith and piety to God, those who were invisible to you when in your world I seemed alone to dissent from all. See now my support, and learn too late how sometimes few may hold fast to truth while thousands err."

"Yes, I will admit to error," returned the professed king, "for I once thought liberty and Heaven to heavenly souls were both the same. But now I see that most, through sloth, would rather serve, inglorious, in cushioned safety."

"Can you be so vain, so foolish," said Abdiel, "to have expected to reach the throne of God unopposed and find it unguarded, his side abandoned at the terror of your power? Fool!—not to think how vain to rise in arms against the Omnipotent, who out of smallest things could raise incessant armies to defeat your folly, or with a solitary hand reaching beyond all limit, with one unaided blow, finish you and submerge your legions in darkness."

"From whence comes this monster hand to crush?" Lucifer scanned the skies in mock alarm. "All I see before me is a herd of sheep and ministering spirits, trained up in feast and song. Such have you armed: the minstrels of Heaven. So let spirits of servility contend with spirits of freedom, and the deeds of both be this day compared and proven."

"Apostate, still you err; nor will you find an end to erring. Unjustly you slander with the name of servitude the worship due him which God ordains. This is servitude," Abdiel accused Lucifer's legions: "to serve the unwise, him who rebels against his worthier, as yours now serve you. Nor are you free, but to yourself enslaved. Seek your reign in Hell; let me serve in Heaven God ever blessed, and his divine commands obey, worthiest to be obeyed. But expect chains in Hell, not realms. Meanwhile, to mark my 'return from flight' as you name it, receive on your impious crest this greeting!"

With this, a noble stroke lifted high and so swift with tempest fell on the proud crest of Lucifer that no quick reflex with shield could intercept it. Ten huge paces did he recoil from the blow—the tenth on bended knee, his balance barely upheld by his massive spear—as if on Earth winds underground or waters forcing way sidelong had pushed a mountain from its seat.

Battle of Angels

AMAZEMENT seized the rebel powers, and heightened rage, to see their mightiest so dazed. His enemies cheered and took it as a sign of victories to come, desire of battle on each side growing fierce. Michael ordered the sounding of the archangel trumpet, and through the vast of Heaven it blew, as the faithful armies shouted praise to God. Nor did the adversaries stand gazing at each other, but joined then in terrible collision. Storming fury rose and clamor such as never was heard in Heaven till now, the sound of mighty armies in pitched battle. Arms clashed on armor, and the madding wheels of brazen chariots roared, as fiery darts hissed overhead in flaming volley. Vaulted with fire, each host rushed against the other with ruinous assault and inextinguishable rage.

Paradise Lost

All Heaven resounded, and had she been then, all Earth would have shaken to her core. And no wonder! —when millions of fierce encountering angels fight on either side, each armed hand a legion in strength, the least of which could wield the elements! Imagine then that power multiplied, army against army, their might limited by their omnipotent King only just short of Heaven's total destruction. Each warrior here led in fight seemed every one himself a leader, expert in judgment when to advance, or stand, or turn the sway of battle, when to open and when to close the ridges of grim war. No thought of flight, nor of retreat—no unbecoming deed betrayed fear. Each relied upon himself, as if in his arms only lay the decision of victory. Wide and varied was the conflict: sometimes a standing fight on firm ground—then, soaring on force of wing, it would ascend, and all the air would become agitated as if on fire.

The battle long hung in even balance, till Lucifer, ranging through the dire tumult, wielding monstrous power, discerned where the mighty sword of Michael struck and felled whole squadrons by its fury. With huge two-handed sway, high its menacing edge would swing and with destruction wide descend. To confront and halt that deadly sword was Lucifer's aim. At his approach, the great archangel desisted from his violent toil, welcoming the opportunity here to end internal war in Heaven by subduing the arch-foe. His countenance all aflame, to the advancing enemy Michael shouted:

"Author of evil—unknown until the crime of your rebellion—these acts of hateful strife will justly fall heaviest upon your own head. Heaven casts you out from all her confines. The seat of bliss does not endure the works of violence and war. Evil go with you and your offspring, your wicked crew, once upright and faithful, now proved false, instilled with your malice; go all to the ordained receptacle of evil: Hell! Take your quarrels there, or let this avenging sword speed your exile with heightened pain!"

"I have sought you specially over all this battle-ground," cried Lucifer, nearing striking range. "Nor will I flee from your utmost force, though it be aided by him called Almighty. Much less expect airy threats to subdue me where with deeds you cannot. Have you turned the least of my followers to flight? —or if to fall, have they not risen again, undaunted? Yet with me you presume to deal more easily—by arrogant words to chase me hence. The strife of glory which you call evil shall not so quickly end. To win is our resolve, or turn this Heaven itself into your fabled Hell, here to dwell forever free, if not to reign!"

Here parley ended, and the two commenced the unspeakable duel; for who, but in the language of angels, can relate this fight; or to what familiar things on Earth compare, that may lift human imagination to such heights of godlike power? Like gods they seemed, in stature and motion—in arms, fit to decide the fate of Heaven's empire. Their fiery swords waved circles in the air; their shields blazed opposite, as two broad suns in terrible expectation of attack. Till now each had met no equal in might. Where moments earlier the battle had been thickest, now lay a spacious field, as from each side the angelic throng withdrew, unsafe within the wind of such commotion. Imagine nature's harmony shattered and war sprung among the constellations.

Paradise Lost

Envision two planetary spheres in dire astrological configuration, rushing in fiercest opposition into jarring combat. Such holocaust in earthly skies would afford weak imitation of these clashing angels.

The contest climaxed when together, with next to almighty force, each uplifted his sword, taking aim for that one stroke which would need no repeat. Neither seemed to have advantage over the other in assault, or in swiftness of defense, but the hard sword of Michael, given him from the armory of God, was so tempered that no substance sharp or solid might resist its edge. Descending steep with force to smite, it met the sword of Lucifer and cut it sheer in half; nor did it stop, but with swift reverse arc entered deep, shearing all his right side. Then Lucifer, the Son of Light, first knew pain. The gaping wound brought him down, contracted and writhing. From the gash, a stream of sanguine nectareous liquid flowed — such as celestial spirits bleed — brightly staining his armor, till his ethereal body, grown of substance not long divisible, closed the wound.

From all sides, angels many and strong ran to his aid. Some interposed defense, while others bore him on their shields back to his chariot where it stood some ways off the main field of action. There they laid him as he gnashed with anguish and disgust and shame to find himself not matchless, his pride humbled by such onslaught, so far had he fallen beneath his confidence to equal God in power. But quickly he healed, for spirits live vital throughout — not as frail man, with entrails, heart, or lung. Spirits cannot, except by annihilation, die. Their liquid texture can receive no mortal wound, no more than can the fluid air. Their being is all heart, all head, all eye, all ear, all mind in one. And they, as they please, assume manlike form, with limbs and wings, in color, shape, or size, as they like best, compact or lucid.

Meanwhile, in other parts of the field took place similar deeds deserving of memorial: as where mighty Gabriel fought and with his forces pierced the solid ranks of furious King Moloch, who with blasphemous tongue threatened to bind and drag him at his chariot wheels, but with shattered arms and hitherto unknown pain, soon fled bellowing, sliced to the waist; or where Raphael and bright Uriel of God's army defeated Adramelec and Asmaden, two potent thrones, huge and armed in rocks of diamond, who disdained to be less than gods but learned harsher thoughts in flight, mangled with ghastly wounds inflicted even through armored plate; or where Abdiel, still prominent in valor, overthrew Ariel and Arioc of the atheist crew, and with redoubled blow, scorched and blasted and stayed the violence of Ramiel. Of thousands might this history relate, and their names here on Earth immortalize, but those elect angels, content with fame in Heaven, seek not the praise of men. As for the doomed opposition, more eager for renown, though wondrous in might and acts of war, nameless in dark oblivion they dwell, canceled from Heaven's sacred memory.

Their mightiest quelled, the battle swerved against the faint satanic host. Surprised by their own fear and sense of pain, their defenses weakened, they soon fled in disorder and disgrace across ground strewn with splintered armor, overturned chariots, and fiery foaming steeds that recoiled, overwearied, those few left standing. In a far different state, the invulnerable saints advanced in unbroken cubic phalanx, impenetrably armed. Such high advantage their innocence gave them above their foes—not to have sinned, not to have disobeyed—that in fight they stood unwearied, not liable to pain or wound, though exposed to heavy acts of violence.

Soon night began her course, inducing darkness over Heaven and imposing a welcome truce. Under her cloudy shelter both victor and vanquished retired, as silence fell on the odious din of war. Michael encamped his angels on the ravaged field, placing watchful cherubic guard by light of waving fire. Lucifer and his rebels withdrew far into the dark plain. Here, dislodged and restless, he called his potentates to council by night.

"Brave companions, we have sustained one day in undecided fight," he began, "and if one day, why not eternal days? What Heaven's Lord has sent against us from his throne, judged sufficient in power to subdue us to his will, has proven not so. May we deem him fallible then, who till now was thought omniscient? Less firmly armed, we did endure some disadvantage, but our empyreal form manifests itself incapable of mortal injury. Our wounds—though severe and inciting pain till now unknown—soon close and heal by natural course. We are imperishable. Our trouble then is small and not difficult to solve. More powerful arms, more violent weapons, will make the odds more equal when next we meet our foes. For this must be where they hold advantage, and surely not in natural prowess. But if other hidden aids bestowed by their Highest Mentor leave them superior still, so long as our sound minds and understanding sense survive war intact, patient search and consultation shall disclose those secrets as well."

Thus concluding, he sat, and Nisroc, highest of the order of principalities, stood next to speak. All wretched from grievous effort, having sustained fierce attack, his tone was bleak:

"Deliverer from new lords, leader to free enjoyment of our right as gods—yet gods who fight in pain, against unequal arms, against unpained, impassive foe—from this must come our ruin, for how can valor exist in pain, which sucks away strength from the hands of the mightiest? Perhaps we could spare all sense of pleasure from our existence and yet live a calm, contented life, but pain is perfect misery, the worst of evils, and when excessive, drains all patience. Pain must end or so does our glorious struggle. Whoever can devise a potent machination to assail our yet unwounded enemies, or invent a defense equal to theirs, to him alone we owe our deliverance."

Lucifer rose but remained silent. He turned his back on the council, oblivious to their concurring murmurs, and gazed across the somber field, whose war-strewn acres had for uninterrupted eons lain unmolested.

"Behold the bright surface of this ethereal soil on which we stand," he finally addressed them, "this wide continent adorned with plant, fruit, ambrosial flower, gems, and gold. The eye but superficially surveys these things, not bringing to mind from whence they grow, while deep underground lay materials dark and crude, of liquid spirits and fiery foam, till kindled with Heaven's ray, transformed, they shoot forth so beauteous, opening to the surrounding light." (The crowd had stilled, puzzled by his distracted comments.) "These elements pregnant with infernal flame we shall draw up from the depths beneath the ground, and in their potent state, ram into hollow engines, which, when touched by fire, shall send forth with thunderous sound among our foes such implements of mischief as will dash to pieces whatever stands opposite. They shall fear we have disarmed thunder itself for our own purpose. Nor does this invention need long labor to build. Dawn shall see our debility end. Brave soldiers, abandon fear and despair and return to thoughts of strength!"

His words ended their dismal mood. All admired the uncanny idea, each wondering how he had missed himself being the inventor, so obvious it seemed once disclosed by their leader. Their joy was narrow-sighted to the imminent need (though all venture for them was doomed by fate), but how much more would they cheer the dire invention when in future days malice should abound, and intent on devilish mischief, they would devise like instruments, their special gift to plague a new enemy on Earth.

Hope revived, innumerable hands were made ready. None stood arguing, but forthwith flew from council to work. In short time they had turned up wide the celestial soil, where beneath lay the sulfurous, nitrous foam that was the crude origin of Heaven's natural abundance. This they extracted, and with delicate skills mixed and heated into blackest grain. After conveying the lethal powder into storage, from hidden subterranean veins they dug up the minerals and stone from which to form their engines and missiles, and then collected the reeds that would carry the fire to kindle the explosive force. All these secret preparations they completed before daybreak.

✝

Across the plain the morning trumpet called the victor angels to arms. In golden armor the radiant host soon banded. From the dawning hills, scouts eyed each quarter to discover where the enemy had lodged, or if they were fled, or in battle march. The distant foe was spotted moving nearer in slow but firm battalion. Zophiel, swiftest winged of the faithful cherubs, came flying back to the garrisoned troops with utmost speed and from midair cried aloud:

"Warriors, arm for fight! The foe believed fled is at hand, saving us long pursuit. In a thick cloud they come, confident and with steadfast resolution. Secure your helmets and grip fast your shields up high, for if these eyes read true, this day will pour down no drizzling shower, but a rattling storm of arrows barbed with fire!"

So warned, they quit themselves of their military baggage and in an instant stood to arms. Embattled, they moved onward, till not far distant the foe appeared approaching in heavy pace, dense and huge. Squadrons deep on every side camouflaged the devilish machinery they hauled. Both armies stood awhile in mutual view, when suddenly Lucifer appeared at the head of his forces and was heard commanding loudly:

"Vanguard, to right and left unfold, that all who hate us may see how we seek truce and with open breast stand ready to receive them. Witness, Heaven, how we freely discharge our part in hope that they accept our overture of peace and not turn away displeased. Appointed, stand by to light what message we put forth—loudly, that all may hear!"

Scoffing in ambiguous words, he scarcely had ended when the front divided and retired to either flank, revealing a triple-mounted row of pillars laid on wheels. Hollowed bodies made of felled oak and fir they were, with ominous gaping mouths. Behind each, a seraph held a reed tipped with fire, which at once all applied to each narrow vent. Opposite, the objects of fire stood entranced and bewildered by the devices new and strange. Upon brief touch of flame, all Heaven lit up, then quickly obscured with smoke, when from those deep-throated engines, whose roar split the air with outrageous noise, a thunderous hail of iron globes descended on the victor host. Struck down they fell who stand otherwise as rocks, angel rolling upon angel, impeded by their own heavy armor, where unencumbered they might have swiftly evaded harm. In forced rout the confused file hesitated, uncertain how to reverse their graceless retreat except to face redoubled overthrow, for in view another rank of seraphim stood in readiness to explode their second thundering volley. Lucifer, enjoying their plight, in loud derision called to his mates:

"Why do these proud victors not come forth? Just a while ago they came on so fierce, but when to receive them we opened wide our overture of truce, straightway they changed their minds, flew off, and fell into somewhat eccentric and ungainly action, as if to dance—perhaps for joy of offered peace."

To which, his clever second in like playful mood added: "Ill-prepared they must have been to receive our propelled treaty standing, for observe how it stumbled and toppled many. How precarious is left all protocol when one's foes walk not upright!"

Beyond all doubt of victory, they presumed to match eternal might with their machines and made scorn of God's thunder, deriding all his host. But the troubled angels did not remain long at bay. Prompted by rage, they found the strength required to oppose such hellish mischief. Forthwith, they threw away their arms and to the rocky hills flew like bolts of lightning and shook those hills from their foundations, loosening to and fro. Such excellence, such power in his mighty angels God has placed, that mountains they upheave at will. Huge rocks and wood were plucked from their firm seat, uplifted and borne aloft by them in hand. Amazement—to be sure—and terror struck the rebel host when coming towards them they saw the bottom of a mountain upward turned. In dreadful awe they watched it fall upon that cursed triple row of engines, and along with these was all confidence under the weight of mountains buried deep. They found themselves invaded next, when on their heads rocky peaks were flung and monstrous boulders of such size that, when in air, whole legions were cast into shadow. Again armor proved more harm than help as, crushed and bent, it bound them painfully in. There was long struggling underneath the avalanche, with many a suffering groan, before they could wind their way out of such prison, spirits once of purest light, made gross by sin.

Paradise Lost

In imitation of their attackers, the rest of their band took up like arms from the neighboring hills. So angels fought in the dismal shade of underground as hill encountered hill amid the air. Earth's war seems a game compared to this uproar of infernal noise and horrid confusion heaped upon confusion. With multiplying rage, these beings of undying stamina might soon have brought all Heaven to waste and ruin had not the Almighty Father, where he sat enshrined in his secure sanctuary, foreseen this tumult and permitted it to pass thus far only that his great purpose might so be fulfilled. For now he would make manifest all his power—transferred to his anointed Son, and upon his enemies avenged.

"Two days are past since Michael and his powers went forth to tame those disobedient," the Lord thus began to him, second in omnipotence. "Their fight has been severe, as likely would it be when two such foes meet armed—for I left them to themselves, powered equally as they were in creation formed, save what sin has now impaired. But that weakness remains imperceptible while yet I forestall their doom; and here might they last in perpetual fight, without termination, with mountains as weapons, making wild work in Heaven, as war performs what war can do. Thus have I permitted two days past; the third is yours, Beloved Reflection of my Glory. For you have I ordained it, that the glory may be yours in ending this great war, since none but you can end it. Now manifest your deserved right by sacred unction, to be Heir and to be King.

"Go then, mightiest in your father's might, ascend my chariot, guide the rapid wheels that shake

Heaven's foundation, and bring forth all my war. Arm yourself with my bow and thunder, and upon your thigh my avenging sword. Pursue these sons of darkness and drive them out from all Heaven's bounds and into the utter deep. There let them learn, as they like, to despise God and Messiah."

Together with this came all meaning too sacred to be spoken, fully expressed in shining rays directed on his son, who rose from the right hand of glory where he sat, and bowing before the Highest Throne, responded:

"Father, Supreme of Heavenly Thrones, First, Highest, Holiest, that you, being well pleased in my deed, might declare your will fulfilled, is my whole delight and purpose. You seek always to glorify your son, as I do you, but whomever you hate, I hate, and can put on your terrors as I put on your mildness. Armed with your might, I will soon rid Heaven of these rebels and drive them down to their prepared ill mansion, to chains of darkness and the undying worm. I now assume your scepter and your power, and more gladly shall resign them back to you when in the end your glory shall be all in all, no comer of Heaven left tainted with disobedience. Then your saints, unmixed from the impure and separated far, shall encircle the holy mount and sing to you adoring hallelujahs, I among them chief."

†

As dawn of the third morning of war in Heaven began to shine, the chariot of God rushed forth with whirlwind sound, flashing thick flames. Steered by no coachman, nor stallion-drawn, it was itself living spirit with instinct, conveyed by four wondrous multi-faced cherubic shapes. Bodies they had like stars, and wings set with emerald eyes. A crystal light hung over their heads, whereon rested a sapphire throne, inlaid with pure amber in rainbow settings. It drew halt before the palace of God, where the Son of Heaven ascended, girded in celestial armor of radiant oraculous gems, work divinely wrought. Beside him hung his bow and quiver stored with three-bolted thunder. From about him rolled fierce effusion of smoke and sparkling flame, as onward he rode.

Far off his coming shone, attended with ten thousand, thousand saints and twenty thousand golden chariots, half on each hand. The great ensign of Messiah borne aloft by angels—his sign in Heaven—blazed far and wide, but was first seen by his own, Michael's command. Surprised by unexpected joy, they stood in awe at his miraculous advance: enthroned in sapphire, riding on the wings of cherubim, sublime in the crystalline sky. Immediately, Michael called back his army, spread wide in battle, and prepared to organize them under their Supreme Head. At the Savior's approach the uprooted hills returned to their place. They heard his unvoiced command and obeyed. Heaven resumed her accustomed face, and hill and valley smiled again with fresh flowerets.

Seeing this miracle, the hapless foes yet stood hard and unrepenting. What signs are of any use to convince the proud or move the stubborn to relent? Without sense or reason, from despair grew desperate hope, and they hardened more by what most should have reclaimed their hearts. The sight of his glory renewed their envy, and aspiring to his height, they rallied their re-embattled powers to fierce rebellious fight, while the Son of God addressed all his host:

"Stand now in bright array and rest this day from battle. Your warfare has been faithful to God and fearless in his righteous cause. But the punishment of this cursed crew belongs to his hand only, or to whose hand he alone appoints. This day's work is not ordained to your multitudes. Stand only and behold God's indignation poured on these godless by me. Not you, but me have they despised and envied. Against me is all their hate. Therefore, to me is their doom assigned. Now they shall have their wish: to try with me in battle which of us proves stronger, they all or I alone against them. Since they measure all by strength of force and aspire to no other scales of excellence, so shall it be. No other merit do I condescend to dispute with them but this, my wrath."

And his countenance changed into terror too severe to behold. At once the cherubic four spread their starry wings, and the orbs of his fierce chariot rolled as with the sound of torrent flood. Downward on his impious foes he drove, gloomy as night. Under his burning wheels all Heaven shook—all but the very throne of God. Soon among them, in his right hand he grasped ten thousand thunders and sent them forth to strike, and striking, infixed in their irretrievable souls the eternal scourge of God. In shock, all their resistance, all courage fell, and down their idle weapons dropped. Over shields and helmets he rode, and helmeted heads of thrones and mighty seraphim, who, lying prostrate, wished the mountains now might again be thrown on them as shelter from his ire. No less violent fell his arrows on either side from the fourfold-visaged four, in which one spirit ruled, where every eye glared lightning and shot forth destructive fire among the accursed, leaving them drained and exhausted and fallen.

Yet he had put forth not half his strength, for he meant not to destroy, but root them out of Heaven. He raised the overthrown and drove them before him as a herd of frightened goats. Relentlessly, to the bounds of Heaven he pursued them with terrors and with furies, till finally the weary flock found its panicky flight stopped at Heaven's end. Here the crystal wall that marks Heaven's border rolled inward and opened wide, disclosing a spacious gap into the black, wasteful deep. The monstrous sight struck them with horror and they reeled backward. But far worse terror urged them from behind. All choice gone, by the thousands headlong they threw themselves down from the verge of Heaven, eternal wrath burning after them into the bottomless pit.

Disburdened, Heaven rejoiced and repaired her separated wall. From the expulsion of his foes, Messiah, sole victor, turned his triumphal chariot homeward to meet his saints, who all stood eye-witness to his almighty acts. Jubilantly they advanced, each bright order shaded with branching palm, and sang praise to him, Victorious King, as he rode triumphant through mid-Heaven into the courts and temple of his Mighty Father enthroned on high, who received him into glory.

Creation

WHEN from his throne God beheld the victorious saints returning, he observed their great multitude and to his Son, their champion, thus spoke:

"You have finished well the rebellion incited by Satan (for so now call him, his former brightness extinguished). Many he drew into fraud, who here know their place no more, but far the greater part, I see, have kept their steadfast station in number sufficient to populate and tend Heaven's wide realm. Still, much of this fertile acreage remains unoccupied, left barren by those unworthy to inhabit here. Now over-ample, this beauteous domain longs to reap the joy of such gentle dwellers for whom it was meant according to ancient plan. Therefore, and so that Satan's heart should not exalt him in the harm he has already done—to have dispeopled Heaven—I can repair that loss, and in a moment create another world.

Paradise Lost

"In that world shall dwell a new race of beings, alike but lesser than the angels. Out of one man, a race of men innumerable shall here first live their lives, until, raised by degrees of merit under long trial, they open for themselves at last the way of God. Then shall their world and Heaven be changed into one kingdom, in joy and union without end."

Great triumph and rejoicing was in Heaven when the Almighty's will was heard declared. Glory they sang to the Most High, good will to future men and peace in their world, and to him glory and praise whose wisdom had ordained to create good out of evil, and rather than linger upon the grieved loss of the unfaithful, to bring into their vacant room a better race, and thus diffuse his good to worlds and ages infinite. To perform these acts of creation in his name, the Almighty delegated his begotten Son.

Between two brass mountains near the temple of God, many thousands of winged chariots harnessed of old had for eons stood in wait for that solemn day now arrived. From the armory of God, spontaneously they came forth, for spirit lived within them. With their advance Heaven's ever-closed gates opened wide, uttering harmonious sounds on golden hinges, moving to let forth the King of Glory on his great expedition to create new worlds. The spoken words of the Father would now be put into effect by the Son, whom he had equipped with equal omnipotence and crowned with the radiance of divine wisdom and immense love. About his chariot poured numberless cherubs and seraphs, potentates and thrones, virtues and all winged spirits. On heavenly ground they stood, and from the shore viewed the vast immeasurable abyss now unveiled:

a turbulent sea, dark, wasteful, wild. From the bottom, surging, mountainous waves turned up with furious winds, as if to assault Heaven's height.

"Silence, troubled waves, and thou Deep, peace," said the Maker. "Your discord end." Uplifted on the wings of cherubim in paternal glory, far into the unborn world he rode, for Chaos had heard his voice and obeyed. All his train followed in bright procession, to behold creation and the wonders of his might. Deep in the black void the burning wheels drew halt, and in his hand he took the golden compasses prepared in God's eternal store to circumscribe this universe and all created things. He centered one point and the other turned round through the vast obscure deep and said, "Thus far extend thy bounds, new World; this be thy just circumference." And over the watery calm the Spirit of God spread his protective wings and infused vital warmth and life-giving essence throughout the fluid mass. And darkness rolled over the face of the abyss.

"Let there be light," said God, and forthwith Light, first of things, sprung from the deep. From her native east, through the airy gloom she began her journey as pure quintessence, sphered in a radiant cloud, for the Sun was not yet formed to contain her. God saw the Light was good, and divided it from the darkness by hemisphere. Light the Day, and darkness Night he named. And so the first day was. Nor did it pass uncelebrated by celestial choirs. When they beheld the orient light first exhaled from darkness, they filled the hollow universe with joy and shout, and touched their golden harps and praised God and his works in hymns, on the first of mornings.

Paradise Lost

✝

Now the universe and the Earth were mixed in calm waters, in matter yet unformed, surrounded by wide crystalline ocean. And God said, "Let there be firmament amid the waters, and let it divide the waters from the waters." And he gathered together all the floating debris, compacting like particles to like, causing to sink downward the cold, black, harsh elemental dregs adverse to life. And out of this mass rose the weightless air, pure, transparent, diffused from every part of the world's raw surface, and above it the designated emptiness of vast airless space, silent and unlit, yet firm and sure separation between the waters of Earth and those of loud Chaos far removed. God called the firmament Heaven, after his celestial city, and the Earth hung therein, self-balanced on her center.

Thus were created the heavens and the Earth, and evening and morning chorus sang the second day.

✝

Again, God said, "Be gathered now the waters under Heaven into their place, and let the dry land appear." Immediately the huge mountains emerged, upheaving their broad bare backs into the clouds, their tops ascending the sky. And as high as were raised the bulging hills, so down sank the roomy hollow bottom, broad and deep. Into this bed the waters rushed headlong, causing the fall of undermined rocks and the rise of walled ridges, such forceful flight his powerful word impressed on the swift flood. As armies at the call of trumpet, so the watery throng charged: if steep, with rushing torrent;

soft ebbing when filling the open plain. Unimpeded by rock or hill, whether underground or in wide circuit, with serpentine meandering they found their way, wearing deep channels in the watery ooze, where henceforth rivers would perpetually draw their humid train and great basins contain the seas. And no sooner had God bid the ground be dry, when all that was not held within these banks became the dry land, earth, and he saw that it was good.

So the Earth was formed, and over all her face main oceans flowed, the womb of waters softening all her globe with warm prolific fluid, her land saturated with generative moisture, coaxing the great mother to conceive. And God said, "Let the Earth put forth grass, herb yielding seed, and the fruit tree yielding fruit after her kind." And the Earth—till then barren desert—brought forth the tender grass which clad her universal face with pleasing green. And herbs of every leaf suddenly flowered, opening their various colors and dispensing sweet smells to her bosom. The clustering vine flourished thick, and melon and pumpkin crept forth; up stood an army of cornstalks in her field; the humble shrub and bush, entwined with frizzled hair, nourished the rivers edge; and the wide tufted valley became all green. Last, the hills were crowned with high woods, where stately trees rose as in dance, and spread their branches, abundant with fruit or budding blossoms.

From all the seas a dewy mist went up, and liquidized, and watered all the ground. The Earth now seemed like Heaven, a seat where gods might dwell or wander with delight. So evening and morning chorus recorded the third day.

Paradise Lost

†

Again the Almighty spoke:
"Let there be lights high in the expanse of Heaven to divide the day from night; and let them be for signs, for seasons, and for days and circling years." And it was so. God made two great lights—great for their use to man—the greater to have rule by day, the less by night. First the Sun, a mighty sphere he framed, first of celestial bodies, though of ethereal mold. Then he formed the moon's globe, and with every magnitude of star, sowed thick the heavens as a field of light, to Illuminate the Earth by night. God saw, surveying his great work, that it was good.

By far the greater part of brightness he placed in the Sun's orb, made porous to drink the liquid light and firm to retain her gathered beams. Here would other stars appear to return, as to a fountain, to draw light in their golden urns. First in the east the glorious lamp was seen, regent of Day, all the horizon round invested with his bright rays. Cheerfully he prepared to run his longitude through heaven's high road, as the gray dawn danced before him. Directly opposite in the west, the less bright moon set her mirror with full face, awaiting night. Borrowing his light, her turn she shined, ascending on heaven's great axle, there to hold reign over a thousand greater lights made less by distance—a thousand, thousand stars that arrived to spangle the hemisphere. Thus, for the first time adorned with their bright luminaries that rose and set, glad evening and glad morning crowned the fourth day.

†

Then God said, "Let the waters generate the living reptile with abundant spawn, and let fowl fly with open wing above the earth in the firmament of heaven." And God created the great whales, and each creeping amphibian which the plentiful waters brought forth by their kinds, and every bird of wing after its kind. And he saw that it was good and blessed them, saying, "Be fruitful, multiply, and fill the waters of the seas and lakes and in the running streams, and let the fowl be multiplied over the Earth."

Forthwith the seas swarmed with large schools of innumerable fish that grazed the seaweed pasture and strayed through groves of coral under the green wave, or with quick leap showed the Sun their glittering coats touched with gold, while others in pearly shells or jointed armor lay in watch under rocks for bits of food that might pass by. Above, the seal and arched dolphin played, and among them, hugest of living creatures, the blue whale, enormous in his gait, turned ocean into tempest, or, stretched like a promontory on the deep, slept or swam, and seemed a moving land.

On cliffs and cedar tops the eagle and the stork built their aerial nests, while from the warm caves and marshes delicately ruptured eggs brought forth numerous fledglings, which soon feathered and soared the air sublime. Some cruised freely the open sky; some with common instinct flew as the prudent crane, in tapering V-formation, and set forth in airy caravan high over land and sea, their way guided by the seasons. From branch to branch, smaller birds fluttered their painted wings and solaced the woods with song till evening, the solemn call of the whippoorwill ceasing not even then. On silver lakes and rivers, the swan bathed her downy breast, proudly mantling her arched neck between white wings, then, quitting the water, rose on stiff pinions, towering the ample sky. On the firm ground walked the crested cock, whose clarion sounded the silent hours, and the amazing peacock, whose bright trains adorned him with the florid hue of rainbow and starry eyes.

The waters thus replete with fish, the air with fowl, evening and morning sanctified the fifth day.

✝

The sixth and last day of creation arose with evening harps and song, and God said, "Let the Earth bring forth cattle and the beasts of the land, each in their kind." The Earth obeyed, and opening her fertile womb, teemed with the birth of innumerous living creatures in perfect forms, limbed and fully grown. Out of the ground, as if emerging from his lair, rose the wild beast in his dwelling place, the forest wild, in thorny thicket and boggy marsh. Cattle ambled forth from among the trees, out to the green fields and meadows—some rare and solitary, some in pasturing flocks and broad herds. Up from the mud the tawny lion appeared, pawing to free his hinder parts, then sprang as if breaking loose from bonds and violently shook his spattered mane. The lynx, the leopard, and the tiger rose like moles, throwing the crumbled earth above them in piles. The swift stag from beneath the ground bore up his branching antlers. And fresh from his vast mold, the hairy mammoth—biggest born of Earth—upheaved his bulk. The wetlands brought forth the creatures that alternate between sea and land: the hippopotamus and scaly crocodile. And from throughout the Earth rose up the bleating of calves and the baying of pups.

Next, at once came forth whatever creeps the ground, insect or worm, and those that wave their limber fans for wings, decked of summer's pride with minute embroidery of gold and purple, translucent azure and green. First crept the frugal ant, joined in common tribes, architects of the underground. Swarming next appeared the female bee, who feeds her husband drone deliciously and builds her waxen cells stored with honey. The rest are numberless to name—not all so tiny, some wondrous in size and serpentine length, and in variety limitless. Trading vital essence with soil, tree, and flowering herb, they covered the Earth.

Now the heavens in all their glory shone and rolled their motions, as the Great Mover's hand first wheeled their course. Earth, perfected in her rich attire, smiled. Air, water, land was flown, was swum, was walked by fowl, fish, and beast in abundance. There remained to be done the masterwork, the end of all yet done, a creature who would walk not prone as the brute, but who, endowed with sanctity of reason, might erect his stature and upright nobly govern the rest. Through his self-awareness he alone would acknowledge Heaven, origin of his being, there to direct his heart with devotion to the Eternal Father, who, omnipresent, now audibly spoke to the Son:

"Let us make now Man after our own image, our counterpart, and let him rule over the fish and fowl of sea and air, beast of the field, and over all the Earth and every living thing that creeps thereupon."

And the Lord God formed man of the dust of the ground and breathed into his nostrils the breath of life. And man became a living soul, created in the express image of God. Male and female he created them, and blessed mankind, saying, "Be fruitful, multiply, and fill the Earth; subdue it, and hold dominion over the Earth and every living thing that moves upon it."

Here he finished, and viewed all that he had made, and beheld all was entirely good. And evening and morning ended the sixth day.

†

Desisting from his work, though unwearied, the Creator returned up to his high throne in Heaven, from there to survey this newly created addition to his empire and to observe how it stood in prospect from his throne, how good, how fair, and whether fulfilling his great conception. Up he rode followed with the sound of angelic praise, ten thousand harps resounding over earth and air. The heavens and all her constellations rang, while the planets in their stations stood listening. The bright host of angels ascended, jubilant, and cried:

"Open, everlasting gates! Let in the great Creator returned from his magnificent work—six days work: a World. Open now, and often from this time hence, for God will wish to visit frequently the dwellings of just men, and will send his winged messengers on many errands of heavenly grace."

So sang the glorious train ascending. Through Heaven's blazing portals opened wide he led them, and direct to God's eternal house, over the broad road whose dust is gold and pavement stars, such as appear to us in the nightly Milky Way. And now on Earth the seventh evening arose in Eden; for the Sun was set, and twilight from the east came on, forerunning night, when at the holy mount the Ordained Maker sat down with his Great Father, who through his omnipresence had accompanied each miracle. Resting from all his work, he blessed the seventh day, the Sabbath, but kept it not in austere silence—for the harp knew no rest, nor the solemn pipe and dulcimer. Sweet sounds rose with clouds of incense from instruments of golden wire, intermixed with choral voices that sang the six days acts:

Great are thy Works, Jehovah; infinite
Thy Pow'r. Behold, thy Empire has no bound.
What thought can measure thee, or tongue describe?
In thy return now greater than that day
From Heaven's Great War won; for to create
Is greater than created to destroy;
Witness, from evil thy Goodness creates
More Good: this new-made World, another Heav'n,
From Heaven-gate not far, founded in view
On the clear Hyaline, the glassy sea
Of amplitude immense, with scattered Stars
Num'rous, and every Star perhaps a World
Of destined habitation; among these,

Paradise Lost

Earth, with her nether Ocean circumfuse'd,
A pleasant dwelling place for happy Men
And sons of Men, brought forth in God's Image,
To worship there and in reward to rule
Over his Works, on Earth, in Sea, or Air,
And multiply a Race of Worshipers
Holy and Just; thrice happy if they know
Their happiness, and persevere upright.

IV

Pandemonium

FROM dazed stupor they awoke, eyes heavy with affliction and dismay, overwhelmed with floods and whirlwinds of tempestuous fire. On all sides flames rose as one great furnace, but from those flames no light issued forth. The fiery deluge fed on ever-burning sulfur that was never consumed. He who was second in power and crime discerned his master by his side in the gloom and broke the ghastly silence:

"Can this be you, great prince, so fallen and so changed, who once outshined bright myriads with your transcendent light? Once joined in glorious enterprise, now we are joined by misery and ruin. Who could have known the force of his thunder?"

"Who indeed!" whispered the companion of his fall, once hailed Lucifer, bright star of Heaven, now Satan his name, as far removed from God and the light of Heaven as one hundredfold the distance from Earth to the outermost star of this universe. Nine days had he and his crew fallen, till Hell at last, yawning, received them whole and closed on them. Around them now through dismal shadows emerged sights of woe and regions of sorrow where peace and rest can never dwell and hope never come. How unlike the place from which they fell, this prison of utter darkness!

"So this is the seat we must exchange for Heaven," Satan continued, "this mournful gloom for that celestial light. So be it. The farther from him the better who is sovereign and will dispose and bid what can be right, not by supremacy of reason, but through force of command." With unrelenting pride and steadfast hate, though in pain, to his battered partner hoarsely he proclaimed: "Neither for this, nor for what else his powerful rage can inflict, will I repent or change! Though outwardly I may be changed, not so in my fixed mind, nor my disdain, nor sense of injustice which raised me to contend with the mightiest. So the field is lost; all is not lost. The unconquerable will, zeal for revenge, immortal hate, and courage never to submit or yield—these remain, and with them I cannot be overcome. His wrath or might shall never achieve that glory over me. To bow and beg for grace on bended knee and worship his power—he who so recently feared for his empire from the terror of my arms—that would be low indeed, disgrace and shame worse than this downfall. By fate we possess the strength and immortality of gods, and through the experience of this great event, stand much improved in foresight. So may we now resolve to wage, by force or guile, irreconcilable and eternal war to our Grand Foe, who now in his sole reign holds the tyranny of Heaven."

"Oh prince of the embattled seraphim," returned his loyal servant of highest rank, him called *Beélzebub*, of darkest fame and basest renown, "too well I see and regret the dire event that has lost us Heaven and in foul defeat laid so low all this mighty host, all glory extinguished, all happiness swallowed up in endless misery. But what if our Conqueror—who now I am compelled to believe almighty, for no less than such could have overpowered such force as ours—what if he has left us our spirit and strength intact only to suffer and support our pains in eternal punishment, that we may satisfy his vengeful ire, or serve as his slaves won in war to do his errands here in the gloomy deep. What advantage then is our undiminished strength or eternal being?"

"Fallen cherub, to be weak is miserable, whether doing or suffering," answered Satan. "But of this be sure: to do good of any kind will never be our goal, but ever the total opposite. Our sole satisfaction will come in resisting and working contrary to his high will. If his plan is to bring forth good out of evil, then our duty must be to pervert that end and out of good still find means of evil."

By now the storm of sulfurous hail that shot after them into the fiery waves where they fell had blown over, and the raging thunder winged with red lightning had spent its shafts and ceased to bellow through the vast and boundless deep. Satan's searching eyes settled upon an area of dreadful desolation, void of light, save what pale glimmer was cast by the livid flames.

Paradise Lost

"It seems the angry Victor has recalled his ministers of vengeance and pursuit back to the gates of Heaven," he said. "Yonder appears a dreary plain, forlorn and wild. Now that his fury is satisfied, let us leave the tossing of these waves and rest there, if rest be possible in this fiery dungeon."

Stretched out huge in length, he uplifted his head above the wave, eyes ablaze, and called strength back into his titanian limbs that extended prone on the burning lake—though never would he have risen from it, or even lifted his head, had not the will and high permission of all-ruling Heaven deigned to leave him at large and to his own dark designs. For with repeated crimes would he heap damnation upon himself while he sought evil to others, and, enraged, see how all his malice served only to bring forth ultimate goodness, grace, and mercy shown on man, whom he would seduce, while on himself he poured treble confusion, wrath, and vengeance. He reared himself upright his full mighty stature, driving the flames backward in rolling billows and leaving in the midst a horrid valley. With expanded wings he steered his flight aloft, weighing heavy upon the dusky air, till he lighted on dry land—if land it could be called, that which burned solid as did the lake with liquid fire. Such resting finds the soles of unblest feet. From on the highest crest, up toward the roof of Hell Satan thrust his loud tribute:

"Farewell, happy fields, where joy forever dwells! Hail, horrors! Hail, infernal world! Let deepest Hell receive her new possessor—one who brings a mind not to be changed by place or time. For the mind is its own place and in itself can make a Heaven of Hell or a Hell of Heaven. What matter where, if I be still the same? Here at least we shall be free. The Almighty has not built this place to be envied and will not drive us from it. Here we may reign secure, and in my mind to reign is worth ambition, though in Hell. Better to reign in Hell than serve in Heaven!"

Next followed his mate, who shared his glory to have escaped Hell's lake as gods, supposed by their own recovered strength and not by sufferance of any heavenly power. From the next hill, where he had lighted, he called to Satan:

"Leader of those armies which none but the Omnipotent could have foiled, see how they lie groveling and prostrate on that lake of fire, astounded and overwhelmed as were we, fallen from such destructive height. If they could but hear that sure voice heard so many times in the thick of battle—calming fears and bringing hope—they will soon revive and find new courage."

Before he had finished speaking, Satan was moving toward the shore. Over the burning soil his uneasy steps gained support from his huge spear, to which the tallest flagship mast hewn on Norwegian hills is but a wand. His ponderous shield tempered in Heaven, massive and round, hung on his shoulders. Through torrid air vaulted with fire, he forced his way to the beach of that inflamed sea, where he stood and called his legions. Broken angel forms they were, strewn thick as autumn leaves across a shaded brook. All the hollow deep of Hell resounded with his call:

"Princes, potentates, warriors, spirits of Heaven, once yours, now lost—if eternal spirits you be, thus confounded with astonishment! Or have you chosen this place after the toil of battle to rest your wearied virtue, or perhaps this is the posture you have taken to adore the Conqueror? So now from above he beholds cherub and seraph rolling in the flood with scattered arms, where his swift pursuers from Heaven's gates, seeing the advantage, may trample you down and with linked thunderbolts transfix you to the bottom of this gulf. Awake! Arise, or be forever fallen!"

Shamed by his words, up they sprung upon the wing, as watchmen caught sleeping at their charge by the dreaded enemy. All pain and preoccupation in their evil plight ceased, and with single mind the multitudes obeyed instantly their general's voice. Numberless were those bad angels seen hovering on wing under Hell's fiery canopy. The uplifted spear of their great sultan directed their course, till they lighted on the firm brimstone, filling all the plain. Forthwith, the heads from every squadron and the leaders of each band hastened toward their commander. Godlike shapes were these, super-human forms, princely dignities, the powers that once sat on thrones in Heaven. Yet in heavenly records no memorial of their names survives, all blotted from the book of life by their foul rebellion. Nor had they yet got themselves new names from the sons of Eve, as would follow them when, wandering over the Earth, they would put man to trial and by falsities and lies corrupt the greater part of mankind to forsake his Creator. Then would they be known to men by various names and various idols throughout the heathen world, transformed to the image of brute, or glitteringly adorned in vain religions full of pomp and gold, devils adored as deities.

Singly they came, according to rank, to where their great emperor stood on the bare shore, while the mixed crowd stayed yet aloof. The first to come forward were those high powers who, long after, roaming from the pit of Hell to seek their prey on Earth, would fix their seats next to that of God, their altars by his altar, adored as gods by all nations wide. Their shrines and cursed images, abominations within his sanctuary, would profane his holy rites and solemn feasts.

First came Moloch, odious king, destined to be besmeared with the blood of human sacrifice and parents' tears, when under noise of drums and timbrels loud, their children's cries would go unheard as they vanished in fire, offerings to his grim idol. For it was he who would by fraud lead the wise heart of Solomon to build his temple against the temple of God on the defamed Mount of Olives.

Next came Chemosh, the obscene, dread of Moab's sons; or Peor—his other name when he would entice the children of Israel into wanton rites, bringing plague upon them and then spreading his lustful orgies even to the hill of Moloch's homicides, till driven by Josiah back into Hell.

Then advanced those various spirits called Baal or Ashtaroth, who would assume both male and female sex as they pleased. For these would the race of Israel often forsake God's righteous altar, bowing lowly down to bestial gods. Among them was Astoreth—later called queen of Heaven—to whose crescent horned image the Phoenician virgins nightly paid their vows and songs. In Zion, on the offensive mount, would stand her temple built by

Paradise Lost

King Solomon, whose heart, though large, would fall—beguiled by his wives—to foul idolatry.

Wanton passions, too, and heat of amorous lament would infect both Syrian damsels and Zion's daughters over the purple river yearly bled by Tammus, who, known to adoring generations as the fair Adonis, next came behind.

Following was one whose brute image his worshipers would mourn when flat it fell in his own temple, maimed by the Lord's fury, head and hands lopped off: Dagon his name, sea monster—part man, part fish—dreaded over the coast of Palestine, king to those hideous elder gods whose sway over Earth's races would ebb and rise across the centuries.

After these, appeared a tribe whose names would be renown in history: Osiris, Isis, Horus, and their train, who with monstrous shapes and sorceries deceived Egypt and her priests. Nor would Israel escape the infection when borrowed gold formed the calf of Aaron.

Last of the highest came Belial, he who loved vice for itself. Never from Heaven fell a spirit more lewd or more gross, or more agreeable to trespass. No temple or altar would rise in his name, yet in all temples and at every altar would his shadow lurk, wherever priest turned atheist, as Eli's sons who filled the house of God with lust and violence. Also would he reign in courts and palaces and in lustful cities where the noise of debauchery and outrage ascends above their loftiest towers. When night darkens the streets, then will the sons of Belial wander forth, spreading insolence and wine, as when the doors of Sodom willingly offered its maidens to avoid worse-threatened rape of men upon men.

Pandemonium

These were the prime in order and in might. The rest are numberless to tell, though far renown—such as the Ionian gods, who would reign throughout the south of Greece, over the fields of Italy and France and the utmost isles of Britain: Uranus and Gala, Titan with his enormous brood, deposed by Saturn, and then mightier Jove. Through smoke, all these and more came flocking with downcast looks, yet also with glimpses of joy to have found themselves not totally lost and their chief not in despair— though his countenance was not without shades of doubt. But these were soon dispelled, for loud sounding trumpets soon recalled his pride as they gave signal that his mighty standard be upreared. That proud honor was claimed by Azazel, a cherub tall, who forthwith from the shimmering staff unfurled the imperial ensign, richly decorated with seraphic arms, whose golden luster when opened to full height shined like a meteor streaming to the wind. At this, the universal host sent up a shout that tore Hell's ceiling. A moment later, ten thousand banners rose into the air, waving bright colors through the gloom, and with them a huge forest of spears and shields in thick array. Forward they moved in perfect phalanx, to the Spartan mode of flutes, like those that raised heroes of old to heights of noblest temper. Those soft pipes had power to charm and assuage troubled thoughts from immortal as well as mortal minds and chase away anguish and doubt, sorrow and pain. With united force and fixed thought they moved on in silent steps over the burning soil, till all stood advanced in full view. A bristling front of dreadful length and dazzling arms, in guise of warriors of old, with stature as of gods, they awaited what command their mighty chief should impose.

Satan's experienced eye darted throughout the armed files, and encompassing the whole battalion across, instantly computed their number. His heart distended with pride, for never throughout the history of war in Heaven or Earth has such embodied force come together in one army. These, whose pride transcends human, now humbly watched and obeyed their dread commander. He stood like a tower above the rest, outstanding in shape and gesture. His form had not yet lost all the brightness of its origin, and he appeared no less than archangel even now, though his glory was obscured, as when the Sun, newly risen, looks through the misty air, shorn of his beams. Darkened so, yet shining above them all, in his face the monarch showed deep scars that thunder had entrenched; care sat on his faded cheek, while under brows of dauntless courage and conscious pride lay waiting revenge. His eye, though cruel, cast signs of remorse and passion to the fellows of his crime, their glory withered, condemned forever to live in pain, millions of spirits paying for his fault—yet how faithful they stood! All his peers bent their double ranks inward from each end, half enclosing him round, and stood in silent attention as he prepared to speak. Three times his voice failed, choked by emotion and stifled tears, till at last words intermixed with sighs found out their way:

"Oh myriads of immortal spirits, powers matchless except by the Almighty: our strife with him was not inglorious, though the outcome dire, as this place testifies. What power of mind from the depth of knowledge past or present could have foreseen how such united godlike force as these which stand before me could ever be repelled? For who can yet believe, viewing these powerful legions whose exile has emptied Heaven, that they could fail even now to reascend, self-raised, and repossess their native seat?

"He who reigns monarch in Heaven sat on his throne upheld by ancient consent, putting forth what appeared to be all his regal state, all the while concealing his full strength. His deception induced our attempt and caused our fall. Now, hence, knowing both his power and our own, we ought not rashly provoke new war, but neither dread whatever war may be waged upon us. It remains for our part to use what strongest powers we have left, namely our will and cunning. Mountains can be moved through fraud or guile sometimes more quickly than by might. So may he learn how victory won by force alone is only half a victory.

"Our fight need not be confined to Heaven, where he practices his advantage, or these gloomy depths. What if space brings forth new worlds? Widespread rumor above held of ancient prophecy that he would create such a world and place there some new kind of creature who should equal in his favor the sons of Heaven. There perhaps shall be our first excursion, if only to pry—there or elsewhere—for this infernal pit will never hold these celestial spirits in permanent bondage. Though peace be forever lost to us, submission is unthinkable. War then! War, open or in subterfuge, must be resolved!"

Out flew a million flaming swords drawn from the thighs of mighty cherubim, confirming his words. The sudden blaze illuminated Hell. With high rage arms clashed against shields, sounding the fierce din of war and hurling defiance toward the vault of Heaven.

There stood not far a hill whose grisly top belched fire and rolling smoke. The rest of its crust shined glossy coated, a sign that beneath lay hidden metallic ore, the work of sulfur. To that place hastened a numerous brigade with winged speed, armed with spade and pick-ax, like a band of soldiers preparing royal camp. By Mammon they were led, least of the high spirits that fell from Heaven; for even there his looks and thoughts were always downward bent to the riches of Heaven's pavement, admiring trodden gold more even than the divine vision of God. By him first would men be taught to rifle with destructive hands the bowels of Mother Earth for treasures better left unearthed. Soon his crew had opened a wide cavity into the hill, where they extracted heavy veins of gold. Let none wonder that riches grow in Hell, for in its accursed soil may best belong that widespread cause of ruin. Further, let those who boast in mortal things, and tell wonderingly of Babel and the works of Egyptian kings, here learn how man's greatest monuments of fame and might and art are easily outdone by spirits—even fallen—and how in an hour is accomplished what they, in a year of incessant toil with innumerable hands, can scarcely match.

On the adjacent plain, a second multitude skillfully melted the heavy ore in many cells prepared over veins of liquid fire fed in through underground channels from the lake. A third, meanwhile, had cast molds of various size and shape within the ground and filled each hollow nook with liquid from the boiling cells. Soon out of the land rose a huge structure. Built like a temple, it was set round with Doric pillars that upheld golden beams, and topped with cornice and sculptured frieze and a roof of fretted gold. Neither Babylon nor Cairo, in all their glories to enshrine their gods or seat their kings, equaled the magnificence of *Pandemonium*, high capital of Satan and his peers.

The tall and stately doors opened to reveal ample space over smooth and level pavement. From the arched ceiling hung rows of starry lamps and blazing torches yielding light as from a sky. The multitude entered, admiring their own work and praising the architect whose hand was known by many a towering structure in Heaven where sat sceptered angels and exalted princes, those the Supreme King ordained to power. His name was also known in ancient Greece and Italy. Men called him Vulcan, the softener of metal, and related in fable how, thrown from Heaven by angry Jove, from morn to noon to summer's eve he dropped from the zenith like a falling star on the Aegean isle of Lemnos. So they told the story, erringly, for he with his rebellious company fell long before. His high towers built in Heaven did not save him, nor his forged machines of war. Along with his industrious crew was he sent headlong, to build in Hell.

By sovereign command the winged heralds sounded their trumpets throughout the host, proclaiming solemn council to be held forthwith. Their signal brought the worthiest from every band and regiment, who came trooping attended with hundreds and with thousands. All access was thronged, gates and porches alike. But within the spacious hall of that

Paradise Lost

infernal court—immense like a covered arena where champions in mortal combat entertain their sultans— the great seraphic lords and cherubim, though numberless, wandered comfortably and discoursed at length on their state affairs, till order prevailed and in close recess a thousand demigods on golden seats prepared for secret conclave. After short silence then and summons read, the great dark council began.

V

Council of the Damned

EXALTED high on his throne of royal state, far outshining Persia's wealth or the riches of India, sat Satan, uplifted from despair, insatiate, and aspiring to further pursue vain war with Heaven. Led by such proud dreams, as yet unseasoned with success, he opened:

"Powers and dominions, fallen deities of Heaven, do not give Heaven up for lost. You can rise again, more glorious and more feared than before your fall, and trust not to repeat that outcome. Justice and the fixed laws of Heaven ordained me your leader and gave you freedom to reign beside me through merit earned in council or in war. At least these rights have been reclaimed and are more securely established in a safe and unenvied throne, yielded to us willingly. High office in Heaven, with its happier state, might draw envy from all inferiors, but who here will covet this highest place, where he who reigns stands exposed foremost against the Thunderer's aim and condemned to the greatest share of endless pain? Here, where there is no good for which to strive, no strife can grow, no dissension or insurrection, for none will want to claim precedence in Hell. None whose portion of present pain is so small will let ambition lead him to crave more.

"With this advantage then, united in firm faith and firm accord, more than can be in Heaven, we will return to claim our just inheritance of old, surer to prosper now than when prosperity was ours. By what best way, then, to achieve our goal, whether in open war or covert guile, we must debate. Who first will speak?"

King Moloch stood, strongest and fiercest rebel spirit that fought in Heaven, made fiercer by despair. His aspiration was to be deemed equal in strength with the Eternal, and rather than be less, would not care to be at all. With that care lost went all fear; of God, or Hell, or worse, he took no heed.

Thus he began:

"Count my vote for open war! I boast no experience in trickery. Let those who have such talent contrive their schemes when time and need allow, not now. For while they sit contriving, the rest, millions, must stand in arms lingering here, impatient for the signal to ascend. Shall these fugitives of Heaven accept meanwhile this dark abusive den of shame for their dwelling place indefinitely, the prison of his tyranny who reigns by our delay? Let us rather choose to force our way all at once over Heaven's high towers, armed with hell-flames and fury, turning our tortures into arms against the torturer. To meet the noise of his almighty power let him hear infernal thunder with rage to equal his, and for lightning see black fire and horror shot among his angels, his throne itself bathed with Hell's sulfur and fire, his own invented torments!

"The way back seems steep and difficult to scale. But is not our more natural motion to ascend on wing rather than descend or fall, as when we sank this far down with such forced and laborious flight, pursued through the deep, our fierce foe hanging on our broken rear? The ascent then, when the sleepy potion of that numbing lake wears off, must be easy by comparison.

"What is there to fear in testing his strength a second time? Can there be some worse way his wrath may find to destroy us? What can be worse destruction than to dwell here, condemned to utter despair in this abhorred deep, where pain of inextinguishable fire must torture us without hope of end. More destroyed than this, we should be quite obliterated; and if our essence be reduced even to nothingness, I say it is preferred over an existence of eternal misery. But if our substance is indeed divine and cannot cease to be, nor our condition worse, what is there to be lost? Our power is sufficient to disturb Heaven's peace, and with perpetual inroads, threaten his inaccessible throne. If not victory, we may at least have our revenge."

So proclaiming desperate battle, he ended, and on the other side rose Belial, in appearance more graceful and humane. A fairer person was not lost by Heaven. He seemed created for high office, but all was false and hollow, for his thoughts were low and vice-ridden. Yet his tongue was sweet and pleased the ear, and he could make the worse appear the better reason and perplex and foil the most experienced council. In his persuasive fashion, with many a well-designed pause and dramatic accent, he claimed all attention:

"I should be as much for grandiose war, my peers, as I am equal to my dauntless comrade, Moloch, in hate, except that the very reasons put forth by him to support that inclination dissuade me most and seem to cast ominous doubt on the whole prospect, for he grounds his courage on despair and utter dissolution, with some dire revenge as the target of all his aim.

"First of all, what revenge can be? The towers of Heaven are filled with armed watch that render all access impregnable. Must we provoke the Almighty Victor to spend all his rage, and that end us? Must that be our cure: to exist no more? Sad cure! For who would want to lose this intellectual being though full of pain, to perish, swallowed up and lost in the wide womb of uncreated night, devoid of sense and motion? And granting that even this result were desirable, who knows whether our angry foe can give it, or ever will? How he can is doubtful; that he never will is sure, for will he, so wise, let loose at once his ire through lack of self-restraint, and unaware, give his enemies their wish and end them in anger, those whom his anger saves to punish endlessly?

"What is our destiny then? Are we cursed to eternal pain? Whatever we do, can we neither relieve our suffering, nor make it worse? But is this truly the worst condition, to be sitting together in this place of our own design, consulting? Have You forgotten our sad flight, when pursued and struck with Heaven's thunder, we sought shelter from the deep? This Hell seemed a refuge then. Or when we lay trapped in the burning lake—was that not worse? What if the breath that kindled those grim fires should reawaken and blow them into sevenfold rage, plunging us back into a deluge of flames? What if all her stores are opened and this firmament of Hell spouts her cataracts of fire upon our heads while we are caught scheming and planning glorious war, and in fiery tempest each she hurls to be transfixed on his rock, the sport and prey of racking whirlwinds, or forever sunk under that boiling ocean, wrapped in chains, there to converse with everlasting groans, unrelieved, unpitied, ages of hopeless end? What folly to believe our state cannot be worsened!

"Count my voice therefore against war, open or concealed. For what effect can force or guile have against him whose eye views all things at once? From Heaven's heights he sees and derides all our vain proposals. No less almighty is he in wisdom to frustrate all our plots and strategies than in his power to resist our force. Shall we then live this vile existence, the trampled race of Heaven, expelled to suffer here these endless torments? Better these than worse, is my advice.

"If we are strong enough to fight, we are strong enough to endure. Our fate is not unjust, nor does it come without forewarning. If we were wise contending against so great a foe, so doubtful what fate might befall us, we should have been prepared for this. How pitiful, when those who are bold and venturous with spear, failing, then shrink with fear and astonishment at what they know must follow: exile, or dishonor, or bonds, or pain—the sentence of their conqueror.

"This is now our doom, and if we can sustain and bear up, in time our Supreme Foe's anger may subside, and perhaps, with us so far removed from his presence and no longer offending him, he may not call us to mind, and these raging fires may slacken as his breath fails to stir their flames. Why should we dread this deep world of darkness? How often does even Heaven's all-ruling Sire choose to reside amidst thick clouds in the majesty of darkness, his glory obscured, while deep thunders roar and play out their rage, and Heaven resembles Hell. Cannot we here imitate his light, as does he our darkness? This desert soil does not lack hidden luster of gems and gold, nor we the skill or art with which to raise magnificent things. And what more can Heaven offer? What is now our torment may eventually become our element, and these piercing fires turn as soft as they are now severe. Our purer essence then will overcome their noxious vapor, or become habituated to it and immune, as our vital temperature evolves more closely to theirs. In time we may adapt to this place in temper and in nature, and receive the fierce heat without pain. Then this horror will grow mild and this dark burden light.

"Who knows what hope the never ending passage of future days may bring—what chance or change worth waiting for? Our present plight seems poor compared to our past, but tolerable, at least safe and tranquil, even good, against the limitless potential for increased horrors which the future holds if we are foolish enough to provoke for ourselves more woe."

He had scarcely finished when a loud murmur filled the assembly—as when hollow rocks retain the sound of blustering winds which all night long rouse the sea. His speech advising ignoble inaction pleased the throng and drew applause, for most of them dreaded a return to the battlefield worse than Hell, so much fear had God's thunder and the sword of Michael wrought within them. Also aroused were their political ambitions and desire to found this lower empire, which through the long process of time might yet compete with Heaven.

With somber aspect then rose Beelzebub, deep deliberation and concern engraved on his brow, his princely face majestic, though in ruin. But for Satan, none sat higher on this council. A pillar of state with the shoulders of Atlas, he seemed fit to bear the weight of mightiest monarchies. His look drew attention still as night.

"Thrones and imperial powers, offspring of Heaven, ethereal virtues, or must we now renounce these titles and changing our style, be called princes of Hell?—for so the popular vote inclines—here to continue and build a growing empire. Wake up from your dreams and know that the King of Heaven has doomed this place our dungeon, not our safe retreat! We live not beyond his potent arm, nor exempt from Heaven's jurisdiction, but remain in strictest bondage and under inescapable restraint, though so far removed. For he, be sure, in height or depth, still first and last, will reign sole king and lose no part of his kingdom by our revolt, but extend his dominion over Hell and rule here with an iron scepter as he does in Heaven with his of gold.

"How then can we sit projecting peace and war? War has been, and this is the result: loss irreparable. No terms of peace are offered or sought, for what peace can the enslaved expect but rigid imprisonment and severe punishment such as pleases their captor? And what peace offering can they return but their hostility and hate? Our only consolation is in revenge, though it be slow coming. We must be forever plotting how best to lessen the Conqueror's success and cut his rejoicing. We need not attempt dangerous invasion of Heaven, whose high walls fear no assault from the deep, if we find some easier enterprise.

"I remind you of that other world, the seat of a new race called *man*, prophesied to be created about this time. Let us learn what creatures may inhabit there, of what shape and substance, and what their strength, and where their weakness. If ancient tradition holds true, they will be of our likeness, though less in power and excellence, but favored more by him who rules above. Though Heaven is shut and Heaven's Highest sits secure in his own strength, this place at the utmost border of his kingdom may lie exposed and left to their own defenses who hold it. Here perhaps some advantage may be achieved by sudden attack, either to waste his whole creation with hell-fire or claim it as our own and drive out the puny inhabitants as we were driven, or if not drive, seduce them to our side, that their God may prove their foe and abolish his own works in anger.

"This would surpass common revenge and interrupt his joy in our damnation, while arousing ours in his disruption, when his darling sons, hurled headlong to share our flames, shall curse their frail origin and faded bliss, faded so soon. Consider then if this be worth attempting, rather than to sit in darkness here hatching vain empires."

The crowd gave loud approval to the devilish plan first devised and proposed by Satan—for where but from the author of all ill could spring so deep a malice to confound the race of mankind and mingle Earth with Hell, done all to spite the Great Creator? Finding the assembly highly pleased by his bold design and with full assent given, Beelzebub resumed:

"Well have you judged and well ended long debate. Great things are now resolved which will once more lift us up from the lowest deep in spite of fate, nearer our ancient seat, perhaps within view of those bright confines, where, when the time is right we may re-enter Heaven, or else dwell in some mild neighboring zone visited with that fair light. There the bright morning beams may purge off this gloom and the soft delicious air breath her balm to heal the scars of these corrosive fires.

"Now let us discover who shall be sent in search of this new world. Who shall we find equal to this journey into the dark unfathomed abyss, to find his secret way through all thick obscurity, or spread his airy flight upward with tireless wings over that vast wilderness? What strength or skill can then suffice to bear him safely through the widespread stations of sentry angels watching round? Here will he need all caution, as no less do we here now in his selection, for on him that we send rests the weight of all our last hope."

Paradise Lost

He sat and awaited who might second, or oppose, or volunteer to undertake the perilous attempt. But all sat silently pondering the danger. Each read in every other's countenance his own dismay that none among the choice and prime of those Heaven-warring champions could be found so hardy as to offer himself to the dreadful voyage. At last Satan rose above his fellows in transcendent glory, and with conscious pride thus proclaimed:

"Oh progeny of Heaven, with good reason are you silent. The way out of Hell is long and hard, for our prison is strong. This huge dome of devouring fire envelopes us ninefold and gates of burning stone bar all exit. Any who makes passage through here is next received by the profound void of formless night—wide gaping and threatening him with utter loss of being, plunged into that abortive gulf. And if his expedition succeeds into whatever world may be, what remains but further unknown dangers and equally hard escape?

"I should ill become this throne if I could be deterred by difficulty or danger from undertaking what is proposed and judged of public importance. By what right could I assume this imperial sovereignty, adorned with splendor and armed with power, yet refuse to accept as great a share of hazard as of honor, equally due him who reigns? Go then, fallen powers of Heaven, tend to what shall be our home and make it more tolerable. Find if there be cure or charm to dull the pain of this ill mansion. Keep watch without break against a sleepless foe, while through all the coasts of dark destruction I seek deliverance for us all. This enterprise none shall share with me."

The monarch thereby discouraged brave show in others who might now volunteer what formerly they feared, certain of his refusal, winning cheaply the high repute which he must earn through real peril. But they dreaded his voice no less than the venture, and all rose, one with him, the sound of their rising resembling remote thunder. They bent in reverence and extolled him as a god, equal to the Highest in Heaven, and expressed admiration that for the general safety he would risk his own. In rejoice over their matchless chief, the council was thus dissolved.

Out into the starless night the grand infernal peers came forth in order — Hell's dread emperor at their middle, imitating godlike state, enclosed by fiery seraphim with bright display and bristling arms. To the four winds, four speedy cherubim put to their mouths the regal trumpets to sound the session's end, and by magic transformation into herald's voice, explain the great result to the waiting masses. Far and wide through the hollow abyss they sent the cry, and all the host of Hell with deafening shout returned them loud acclaim.

Lest men boast their deeds on Earth, excited by glory or ulterior ambition, let them know how devil with devil holds firm concord, while of all rational creatures only men find cause for endless dispute, proclaiming peace before God, yet living in hatred and strife among themselves — waging cruel and perpetual war, wasting the Earth to destroy each other — as if man did not have enough hellish enemies that day and night lay in wait for his destruction.

VI

Man

HIS CHEST swelled abruptly with much needed air, his first, sucked in by a gasp. Out it passed in a sigh, as straight toward Heaven his eyes turned and gazed awhile at the calm, spacious sky. He lay in balmy sweat, which the Sun's warm ray soon dried. Soft flowery herbs made his bed; but restless instinct soon raised him from dreamy repose. Up he sprang and upright stood on steady feet. About him he saw hill, dale, shady woods and sunny plains, and water falling in murmuring streams. Nearby there were creatures that lived and moved, walked or flew. Birds warbled on branches, all things smiled with fragrance, and his heart was filled with joy.

He turned his wandering eyes upon himself, and limb by limb perused, and testing his supple joints, walked, and sometimes ran, urged by lively vigor. But who he was, or where, or why, he knew not. He tried to speak, and succeeded. His tongue obeyed, and he found he could readily name whatever he saw. "Sun," said he, "you who enlighten all the Earth, so fresh, and hills and dales, rivers, wood and plains, and you that live and move, fair creatures, tell me if you saw how I came to be. If formed by some Great Maker, tell me how I may know him by whose work I move and live and feel that I am happier than I know."

He strayed far from that place where first he drew breath, and finding his uttered questions brought no reply, sat down pensively on a green shady bank profuse with flowers, where drowsiness overtook him. He thought he would pass into his former state, insensible, this brief Heaven dissolved, when suddenly to his inner vision, circumventing need of eyes, appeared one of divine shape, who spoke to him:

"Rise, first of men. It is I whom you have sought, author of all you see, who have come to guide you to your prepared place in the garden of bliss. Your mansion awaits you, Adam."

Then by the hand he raised him and led him over field and valley to a woody mountain whose top enclosed a broad plateau, richly planted with charming walks and arbors and crystal cascades. What Adam had seen of Earth before scarcely seemed pleasant compared to this. Each tree hung laden with fairest fruit, tempting to the eye. Sudden appetite stirred in him to pluck and eat, but he withheld.

"This Paradise I give to you, Adam, father of men," said the Divine Apparition, "to till and keep, and of the fruit to eat. Of every pleasure herein, with glad heart may you partake; no desire you may know shall here go unfulfilled. Fear no want in this place. Of every tree that grows in this garden, eat freely, but for one. In the middle of the garden by the Tree of Life, I have set the tree which brings knowledge of Good and Evil. Here it tests my pledge of your obedience and faith. Shun its taste, for with it comes bitter consequence. Remember this warning: On the day you shall eat of that tree, my sole command do you transgress. Then inevitably shall you die the death. From that day mortal, you shall lose this happy state and be expelled from this into a world of pain and sorrow."

Sternly he pronounced this rigid prohibition, which would thenceforth chillingly resound in Adam's ear, but soon continued, more mild, to complete his gracious purpose: "Not only these fair bounds, but all the Earth I give to you and your race. Possess it as lords and rule over all things that live therein, in sea or air, beast, fish, and fowl."

As the Lord departed, Adam cried after him: "Heavenly Vision, Benign Giver of all things fair, all these gifts I receive, overjoyed, these wondrous works set before me, with only one restriction in all the world. Never will I break this one commandment, easy to keep; for one delight denied amid so much bounty will go unmissed. Folly it would be to risk all this for one indulgence—great loss at such small gain. But were the loss great or small, still would I strive to obey and please my kind Master."

Exploring his Paradise, Adam found it brimming with all forms of living things. And as he went he named them, each and every kind, and understood their nature, for God had endowed him with sudden apprehension. But in all these he found not what he sought.

When night fell he lay upon the ground, transfixed in melancholy fascination by the crescent moon and drifting stars, till God brought a deep sleep upon him. Stooping where he lay, the Creator opened Adam's left side and took from there a rib, warm with vital life-blood streaming fresh. Wide was the wound, but Adam stirred not, and quickly it was filled up with flesh and healed. The rib the Maker formed and fashioned with his hands, and under his forming hands a creature grew.

In Adam's sleep, visions reshaped and enlarged the familiar elements of nature upon a spacious landscape. It seemed he walked about a spreading terrain, whose vastness diluted all natural joy. The air was laden with silence, and the forlorn fields craved living voices to fill the hollow. From a bevy of sparrows erupted a frenzy of chirping that broke his wistful dream, rousing him in time to attend the Sun's glorious re-entry into Paradise. Day renewed the evolving enigma of some felt flaw in his perfect world. But when he encountered the Lord walking in the garden, he fell on his knees, ejaculating effusive greetings:

"Oh Great Maker, Author of this universe, amply you have provided all things good to man and his well-being! No place could hold beauty more abundant to delight the eye, or fragrance sweet, or soft sounds that soothe the ear, or warmth of golden ray or cool of brook to comfort the flesh, or succulent fruits in such varied color and taste that please the appetite!"

"Adam, such heavy praise casts a shadow of unspoken discontent," said the Lord. "What pleasure is it you lack among all these prescribed?"

"Master," he answered, startled by God's wisdom, "every manner of pleasure have you assigned for my sole enjoyment." Here he rose and followed a pace or two behind the Lord, who resumed his tour. "But—what happiness can be in solitude? Who can enjoy alone, or alone find contentment in all the wonders of Paradise?"

"What do you call solitude?" said God. "Is not the Earth populated with various living creatures, the air and sea as well, and these all at your command?"

"The fellowship I seek is the sort that can participate in rational exchange of thought," Adam replied, "and share its delight. The brute cannot be companion to man, but rejoices, each with his kind, as you have so rightly paired them: lion with lioness, but not bird with beast nor fish with fowl nor ox with ape. Least of all then can man with beast find consummate friendship."

"You are as a king on Earth," said God, "and they your subjects who worship you. They are marvelous in their complex natures, nor are they lacking in natural wisdom. Do you not know their language and their ways, and do they not come and play before you at your call? With these may you find pastime and bear rule, for your realm is large."

"Heavenly Power, I marvel at the creatures of the land and sea and delight in their charm. But you have made me here your deputy, and these made inferior and set far beneath me. Can social intercourse find harmony or true delight among unequals? Must not society be mutual and in due proportion given and received? For otherwise, one dominant and the other submissive, the inequality cannot sit well with either, and such company soon proves tedious for both." With youthful candor, Adam pursued debate against the Highest Wisdom, so mild was the Lord in his company.

"What then of me, Adam, and this my state?" asked God. "Do I seem to you not possessed of enough happiness?—for I am alone from all eternity. There are none second to me, nor like me, much less equal to me. With whom do I have to converse other than the creatures which I make, which are inferior to me by infinite measure greater than are these to you?"

But Adam persisted, searching words to hold such argument as spontaneous insight brought forth:

"To attain the height and depth of your eternal ways, all human thought comes short. In your secrecy, although alone, you are best accompanied. No outside communion can add to your omniscience, though you can, if you please, raise your creatures to what height you will and make them like gods. But I cannot by conversing cause these beasts to stand erect and walk beside me. You are perfect in yourself and without flaw. Not so with man; his defects are many. But, through interaction with his kind, each may learn to raise his condition by degrees, or bring solace in affliction. There is no need that you should propagate; you are already infinite and through all numbers absolute, though one. But man must manifest his potential in numbers great. No one man can be but a particle to human achievement. Each man, imperfect in his oneness, requires aid, understanding, encouragement in his striving, and cheering praise of success achieved. Alone he is static; he must move in parallel unions of love and friendship to make him whole in his being."

God smiled. "Thus far I am well pleased in you, Adam. You know not only of the beasts, which you have rightly named, but of yourself, and have well expressed the free spirit within you. With good reason should you disdain fellowship with brute beasts. I have not imparted my image to them, and they are therefore not fit companions for communion with you."

Adam sat, exhausted, his human sense strained to its height, over-awed by the sublime celestial discourse. Dazzled and spent, he drowsily pondered —as if recalling another's words—the wisdom of those which, through intuitive knowledge, had been borne by his own lips.

"Before you spoke, I knew it was not good for man to be alone," continued the Lord, "and did not intend for you to be left with only such company as you see around you. What next I bring shall please you, be assured: your likeness, your help, your other self, your wish—exactly as your heart desires."

✝

She awoke and found herself reposed upon flowers under a shade, much wondering where and what she was, and how she came to be. From not far distant came a murmuring sound of waters issued from a cave and spread into a liquid plain, where they stood unmoved, pure as the expanse of blue above. There she went, drawn with unexperienced thought, and laid herself down on the green bank to

Paradise Lost

look into the clear smooth lake that seemed another sky. As she bent down to look, just opposite, a shape within the watery gleam appeared, bending to look up at her. She started back, it started back, but pleased, she soon returned. It returned as soon with answering looks of sympathy and love. There would she have fixed her eyes and pined with incessant vain desire, had not a voice warned her:

"What you see, fair creature, is but a shade of yourself. With you it comes and goes. But follow me and I will bring you where one who is more than shadow awaits your coming and your soft embraces. He whose image you are shall you enjoy, inseparably yours. To him shall you bear multitudes like yourself and be called mother of the human race."

She followed straight, invisibly led, till she espied him under an elm tree. Fair he was indeed and tall, but less fair, she thought, less soft or amiably mild than that smooth watery image. Back she turned. He followed and cried aloud, "Return, fair Eve. Who do you flee? Who you flee, of him are you made—his flesh, his bone. To give you being I gave life out of my side, the side nearest my heart, to have you by my side always. You are part of my soul, my solace, my other half."

His gentle hand seized hers, and she yielded.

VII

Journey to Earth

ONE seemed a beautiful woman to the waist, but below became scaly in folds and coils, a writhing serpent armed with mortal sting. About her middle raced a pack of snapping hell-hounds that barked loud and unceasingly. If frightened, into her womb they would creep, yet still bark and howl unseen within. The other shape, if shape it could be called, having no distinguishable limb or substance, stood black as night, huge and fierce and terrible as Hell, and shook a menacing dart. Upon what seemed his head sat the likeness of a kingly crown.

Satan was now at Hell's boundary. In solitary flight had he scoured each coast, sometimes on shallow wing roaming the frightful depth, then soaring the towering cavern high, till at last appeared Hell's portal, held fast and impenetrable by threefold gates of brass and iron and adamantine rock, high reaching to the fiery roof. There, on either side sat these two formidable shapes. From his seat the formless monster moved forward to meet the oncomer, Hell trembling at his horrid strides. But Satan, who feared no created thing, stood fast, undaunted though astonished at the terrible specter.

"What accursed shape dares block my way to Hell-gate?" he demanded. "Through here I mean to pass, be assured, grim shadow. Retreat or taste your folly and learn by proof, Hell-born thing, not to contend with spirits of Heaven."

To which the goblin, full of wrath, replied:

"Are not you that outcast traitor angel who first broke peace in Heaven, attempting war against the Highest? By what right do you yet link your name with that place which disgorged you, and here breathe defiance where I reign king?—your king and lord, since you are here and not there. Back to your punishment, Hell-doomed fugitive, and add wings to your speed lest I spur your lingering with a whip of scorpions, or inflict with one stroke of this dart pangs unfelt by you before!"

As he spoke his threats, the grisly terror grew tenfold more deformed and dreadful, while before him Satan burned like a comet, incensed with indignation. The frowns cast between them foretold an impending storm—as when two black clouds charged with Heaven's artillery come rattling over the sea and stand front to front. Hell grew darker at their encounter, So mightily matched they stood, neither likely again to meet so great a foe. Each leveled his deadly, aim at the other's head, their fatal hands intending no second stroke. Now dire conflict would have rocked all Hell, had not the snaky sorceress that sat fast by Hell-gate risen (for it was she who kept the fateful key), and with hideous outcry leapt between them like a striking cobra:

"Father, stay your hand! Would you slay your only son? Son, what fury possesses you to wield that mortal dart against your father's head—while he who sits above laughs at you both?"

The monster paused, and Satan froze at such strange outcry from the double-formed she-thing.

"Why do you call me father," he asked, "and that phantasm my son? I know you not, nor ever saw till now a sight more detestable than him and you."

"Have you forgotten me then?" the portress of Hell-gate replied. "Do I seem so foul in your eyes now, where once my form bred pleasure and satisfaction?

"Recall to mind that time above, at the assembly of your followers, who joined with you in bold conspiracy against Heaven's King, when suddenly intense pain surprised you and dimmed your eyes. Your head threw forth thick flames and opened its left side wide, giving me birth. I rose, a fair goddess bright, in sight of all the host, who recoiled in amazement, afraid at first. They thought me a bad omen, and called me *Sin*. But soon I won them with my attractive graces, and none did I please more than you, my sire, who saw yourself reflected in me. Enamored, you took your pleasure with me in secret, and from that union my womb conceived a growing burden.

"Meanwhile war arose, resulting in that cata-clysmic fall of you and all your host, me among them, driven headlong from the pitch of Heaven down into this deep, at which time this powerful key was given into my hand by Heaven's emissary with charge to keep these gates forever shut. Here I sat alone till in my womb, made pregnant by you and now grown excessive, I felt monstrous movement causing me torturous pain. At last this odious offspring you see before you, your own begotten, broke way, tearing through my entrails with such violence that my lower parts grew distorted and transformed into this serpentine shape. He issued forth, brandishing his fatal dart made to destroy. I cried out, *'Death!'* Hell trembled at the hideous name and sighed from all her caves, and back resounded: *'Death!'*

"I fled in fear but he pursued, inflamed more with lust than rage it seems, for he overtook his mother and lay with me in forced embrace. Of that foul rape were born these yelling monsters that surround me with ceaseless cry, reconceived and reborn hourly, to my unending agony, for as they choose they return into the womb that bred them, and howl, and gnawing there, feed on my bowels, then burst forth with rebirth of terrors to torment me without rest or relief.

"Before my eyes sits grim Death, my inbred horror, my son and sorrow, who would soon devour them and me, his parent, for want of other prey, if he did not know that his survival links with mine, for I would prove a bitter morsel and his poison. So Fate pronounced. But father, I warn you, shun his deadly arrow. Even those bright arms tempered in Heaven will not render you invulnerable to that mortal stroke."

She finished, and the revealed sire of this unholy trinity surveyed his family. "Am I to believe this abomination my son," he said, "result of that sweet joy had with her in Heaven, who now, so sadly altered, calls me father? But why should I expect to find change less dire in you than that befallen me and all my host—changes all unexpected, unforeseen, unthought-of.

"Know then, dear daughter, that I come as no enemy, but to set free out of this dismal house of pain both him and you and all the spirits that fell with us from Heaven. For them I venture forth alone into the void to search a place foretold wherein a race of new creatures is raised, perhaps to fill our vacant room. If this be so—and what more this secret involves—I seek to know. Then I will return and bring you to the place where you and Death may dwell at ease. There may you move about freely and unseen, and each be fed and filled unceasingly, for all things shall be your prey."

Death grinned a ghastly smile and stroked his bloated stomach, to hear his famine should be soon ended. No less pleased, his evil mother fondled the dreadful key that hung at her side.

"What do I owe to the commands of him above who hates me?" said she, "who thrust me down into this profound gloom, confined to sit in hateful duty, with perpetual agony and pain. You are my father, my author; you gave me being. Whom should I obey but you who will bring me to that new world of light and bliss among those who live at ease, where I shall reign in luxury at your right hand forever, as befits your daughter and your love."

Then rolling her bestial train towards the gate, she drew up high the huge grating, which all the infernal powers could not have moved. Into the keyhole she slid the instrument and turned the intricate tumblers till every bolt and bar of massive iron and solid rock unfastened with ease. Violently the huge doors flew open with jarring sound, grating harsh thunder on their hinges that shook the bottom of Hell, till they stood open so wide a bannered host with horse and chariot ranked in wide formation might pass through with ease. Like the mouth of a giant furnace, the opening overflowed smoke and flame.

Before their eyes in sudden view appeared the secrets of the ancient deep—the womb of nature and perhaps her grave: a dark illimitable ocean, without bound, without dimension, where length, breadth, and height, and time and place are lost—where heat, cold, water, and air struggle fiercely for mastery, and bring into battle their unborn atoms, unnumbered as the African sands, tossed by warring winds in eternal anarchy. To whom these most adhere, he rules for a moment. Chaos sits umpire, and by decision further embroils the fray; next him, high arbiter, Chance, governs all. Here the elements, mixed confusedly in their pregnant causes, must thus ever fight until the Almighty Maker ordains them his dark materials with which to create more worlds.

The wary fiend stood on the brink of Hell and looked awhile into this wild abyss, pondering his voyage. It was no narrow river he had to cross. From beyond the portal rose noises loud and ruinous, no less than if this cosmic frame we inhabit were to collapse, and the elements in mutiny tear the steadfast Earth from its axis.

At last he spread his broad wings for flight and ascended into the surging smoke. Many a league he rode recklessly amid the swirling clouds, till unawares he found himself plunged into a vast vacuum. Vainly he beat his wings against nothingness as he dropped straight down ten thousand fathoms, and to this hour might yet fall had not by ill chance the updraft of some tumultuous cloud charged with fire and nitrate caught and carried him as many miles aloft. That cloud's fury ended in a region of boggy mire, neither sea nor solid land, where the fluid terrain required him to tread the crude substance half on foot, half flying, to escape engulfment. So the fiend, over bog or chasm, through regions dense or rare, against torrent rush or vacuous stream, with head, hands, wings, or feet, swam or sunk, or waded, or crept, or flew—yet steadfastly pursued his unknown way.

Boldly he explored the secrets of the realm, half-lost, alone and without guide, till at length a sudden hubbub of wild sounds borne all confused through the hollow dark assaulted his ear with loudest vehemence. Rumor and his consort, Chance, Tumult and Confusion stirred up from the wasteful deep, and Strife, with a thousand various mouths, were all immersed in a dreadful brawl that quickly swept him up in its irresistible force. Helpless, he was hurled between jostling boulders of ice and clay at hurricane force, till the wind's centripetal fury plunged him into its empty core, where he was hit by a blast of silence.

Free floating in the whirlwind's eye, he anchored himself to a weightless mass and took the advantage to collect his balance. Quick intermission it might be, for in the physics of anarchy the encasing tornado could dissolve without warning, or instantly collapse, or explode, sending him inexorably back into Hell. In the weird, black quiet, he considered what little chance he had to discover the new world through random search. If God invented his new creation to greater glorify himself, then, unlike the Hell that stretched far across the bottom of this nethermost abyss, must not he have placed his favored world— Heaven's offspring—comfortably near at hand, where from his idle seat he might gaze lovingly upon it in amusement and self-admiration? To Light then— for Heaven is Light—must he upward tend to hunt the nearest coast of darkness.

"Powers of Chaos, guide me onward!" he cried out in the echoing wind chamber. "For my mission is to spread havoc and spoil and ruin—your gain and dark kingdom restored, so late encroached upon by other worlds!"

With fresh alacrity and force renewed, up he sprung like a flaming meteor through the shock of fighting elements on all sides round, and upward flew into the wild expanse—upward and toward whatever source he could perceive of those few droplets of surviving light that trickled through the cluttered void, as they meekly sought the way of least resistance.

Slowly, with his advance, the sacred influence of light increased, issuing from the walls of Heaven a glimmering dawn, shooting far into the bosom of dim night. Here Nature first begins her farthest verge, as from his outmost works Chaos slowly retires, a broken foe, with diminishing fury and less hostile din. Now by unsteady light, Satan glided with ease on the calmer wave, like a weather-beaten vessel gladly making for port. In the emptier, air-like waste, he hung on spread wing, pausing to behold at leisure the far off empyreal Heaven, once his native seat, its opal towers and battlements adorned with vivid sapphire. There, beside the mother planet, resembling a star of smallest magnitude beneath the moon, as on a golden chain from Heaven's luminous globe, hung this pendant universe.

†

From his high prospect, wherein all past, present, and future comprise his view, the Almighty Father bent down his eye and beheld our first parents on Earth reaping the immortal fruits of joy and love—uninterrupted joy, love unrivaled—while in the gulf between them and Hell, Satan coasted the wall of Heaven in the sublime twilight air, ready to swoop down with wearied wings on the bare outer shell of this universe.

"See what rage transports our adversary," said God to his only son, who sat radiant at his right hand. About them all the saints of Heaven stood thick as stars. "No bounds or bars of Hell, nor wide abyss can hold him, so bent he seems on desperate revenge. He wings his way direct towards the new created world to test whether man placed there can be destroyed by force, or worse, perverted by some treacherous deceit.

"His venture will succeed, for man will be fooled by his flattering lies and easily transgress the sole commandment. So will man and all his faithless children fall through none but his own fault. He has from me all he can have; I made him just and right, strong enough to stand though free to fall, just as I created all the spirits of Heaven—both those who stood and those who failed. Freely they stood who stood, and fell who fell. Not free, what proof could they have given of true allegiance, or constant faith, or love sincere? What pleasure could I know, what praise could they receive for obedience paid by compulsion, without will or reason? Such obedience serves necessity, not me. Therefore were they created free, both man and angel, authors to themselves in all they judge or choose. Free I formed them and free they must remain till they enslave themselves.

"But since man falls through deception by the archenemy—whereas he and his legions fell by their own corruption, self-tempted, self-depraved—man therefore shall find grace, the other none. Through Heaven and Earth shall my glory excel in mercy and justice, but mercy first and last shall brightest shine."

Tears fell through all Heaven at the news of man's impending fall, but that sadness was mitigated by a sense of new ineffable joy that was diffused like ambrosial fragrance among the blessed spirits by the divine compassion uttered.

"Man shall not quite be lost," the Lord continued, "but saved, some, who hear me call to warn of their sinful state. Often shall they hear me call. I will clear their senses of the dark and soften stony hearts to pray, repent and bring obeisance due. And if endeavored with sincere intent, my ear shall not be slow, my eye not shut. Once more shall they stand on even ground against their mortal foe, upheld by me, that they may know how frail their fallen condition is, and that to me they owe all their deliverance, and to none but me. And I will place within them as a guide, conscience, which if they will hear, light after light shall they attain, and persisting to the end, safe arrive.

"They who neglect and scorn my word shall never taste my day of grace, but hard be hardened, blind be blinded more, that they may stumble on and deeper fall. These only shall I exclude from mercy and none other.

"But mercy alone will not save man, who disobeys and breaks his fidelity with me, reaching for godhood and so losing all. Nothing can amend his treason. He is doomed to vowed destruction, and with him his whole posterity must die. They die or justice does, unless some other willingly pays the rigid penalty in their place: his death for man's salvation. Speak, heavenly powers, where shall we find such love? Which of you will become mortal to redeem man's mortal crime? Does any such charitable spirit dwell in all of Heaven?"

But all the heavenly choir stood mute, and silence was in Heaven. No intercessor appeared on man's behalf, much less one who would draw upon his own head the deadly forfeiture and ransom set. And now without redemption would all mankind have been lost, doomed to death and Hell, unalterably, had not then spoken the Son of God:

"Father, your word has passed that man shall find Grace. Then shall not Grace find means to find her way to man?—she who visits all your creatures, speediest of your winged messengers, who comes to all unasked. And how can man ask, once dead in sins and lost? Indebted, no atonement has he to offer for himself. Behold me then! Me for him, life for life I offer. On me let your anger fall. Account me man. For his sake will I leave your bosom and freely put off this glory enjoyed next to you, to suffer and die for him. On me let Death wreak all his rage. Under his gloomy power I shall not long lie vanquished. You have given me to possess life in myself forever. Though I yield to death all of me that can die, that debt once paid, I shall not dwell with corruption in the loathsome grave, but rise, victorious, and subdue my vanquisher. Death his death's wound shall then receive, disarmed of his mortal sting, and with his carcass the grave will receive its fill, while all Hell becomes my captive, all the powers of darkness bound. At this sight shall you look down out of Heaven and be pleased. Then, with the multitude of newly redeemed souls, I will re-enter Heaven to see in your face no cloud of anger, but peace returned and reconcilement assured. Then wrath shall be no more, but in your presence entire joy."

His words ended, yet even in silence his meek expression spoke immortal love to mortal men. Admiration filled all Heaven that such high sacrifice was so gladly offered to attend the will of the Great Father, who thus responded:

"Son and source of my greatest joy, you are the only peace found for mankind under wrath. You know how dear to me are all my works, man not the least, though last created. For him I spare you from my bosom and right hand, that by losing you a while, the whole race is not lost. Go therefore and join your nature to his when the time shall come and be yourself made flesh, man among men on Earth. Take then Adam's place as head of all mankind.

As in him all men perish, so in you shall they be restored—as from a second beginning.

"In Adam's hands I have placed sole charge to prove the worthiness of his race. By his test all humanity is put under trial; thus, his crime places guilt on all his sons. But your goodness shall absolve those who renounce their own unrighteous deeds and live reborn in you. So man, as is most just, shall atone for man, be judged and die, and dying, rise, and rising, with him raise his brethren, ransomed with his own dear life. So heavenly love shall outdo hellish hate, yielding to death and dying to redeem what hate so easily destroys.

"Because you offer to quit your high throne equal to God and descend to assume man's nature—quitting all to save a world from utter loss—you are found worthiest to be Son of God, by merit more than by birthright, by being good far more than great or high. Because in you love has abounded more than glory abounds, therefore your humiliation shall exalt your manhood with you also to this throne. Here shall you sit embodied; here shall reign both God and Man, Son both of God and Man, anointed universal King. All power I give you; reign forever and assume your reward. To you all knees shall bend of those that dwell in Heaven, or Earth, or under Earth in Hell.

"And when at last the summoning archangels are sent to proclaim your dreaded final judgment, forthwith from all winds the living and the summoned dead of all past ages shall hasten to the general doom, such a peal shall rouse their sleep. You shall appear in the sky, gloriously attended. Then with all your saints assembled, you shall judge bad men and angels, who, accused, shall sink beneath your sentence. Hell, her numbers full, shall thenceforth be forever shut. Meanwhile, the world shall burn, and from her ashes shall spring a new Heaven and Earth, wherein the just shall dwell, and after all their long tribulations, see golden days, fruit of their golden deeds, triumphing with joy and love and truth. Then shall you lay down your regal scepter, having no more need, for God shall be all, and all in God.

"But now all ye sons of Heaven, adore him who gives his life that this may come to be. Adore the Son, and honor him as me."

No sooner had the Almighty ended, but all the multitude of angels filled the eternal regions with a shout loud—as from numbers without number—and sweet—as from blessed voices uttering joy. Heaven rang with jubilee and loud hosannas. Towards either throne they bowed and to the ground cast down their golden crowns in solemn adoration. Then, crowned again, they took their golden harps, ever-tuned, that hung like quivers glittering by their side, and sang their sacred song that wakened raptures high: first, to the Father Omnipotent, Immutable, Immortal, Infinite, Eternal King, Author of all being; next, to the Son, who offered himself to die for man's offense, and thereby end the strife between mercy and justice that marred his father's perfect brow.

"Oh unequaled love," they sang, "love nowhere to be found less than divine! Hail, Son of God, Savior of Man! Thy name shall henceforth abound in my song, and never thy praise shall my harp forget, nor thee glorify less than thy father!"

†

Meanwhile, upon the firm dark globe of this off-spring universe walked Satan, newly alighted. A tiny jewel far off, now it seemed a boundless continent, dark and wild. On this dense shell walked the fiend as on a spacious field, while enclosed within and divided from Chaos hung unseen luminous spheres, numberless as the spirits of Heaven. Order and perfect balance reigned within, while without all stood exposed under perpetual starless, inclement night, ever-threatened with storms of Chaos blustering round, except on that side which gained some small reflection from the distant wall of Heaven. There the air glimmered, less troubled with loud tempest.

Bent on his evil errand, up and down this untrod wasteland Satan stalked—as does the vulture that lights on the barren desert on his way from the mountain scarce of prey to the hills where flocks are fed, there to gorge the flesh of lambs or newborn kids. Alone he wandered, for on this dark plain no living creature was to be found. At last a gleam of dawning light turned his weary steps. Far in the distance loomed a magnificent structure, ascending by degrees the high wall of Heaven. At the top appeared the way of entry, framed in work more rich than any kingly palace gate. Thick with sparkling gems the portal shone, its panels embellished in diamond and gold, impossible to match by earthly model. The stairs were those whereon Jacob saw angels ascending and descending when he dreamed under the open sky in the fields of Bethel. Underneath flowed a bright sea of jade and liquid pearl. Those who later came from Earth would arrive sailing, or floating above the lake, transported in angel-drawn chariots. Here would wait Saint Peter with his keys at the top of the steps, which now hung unattended, in open view, as if to dare the fiend attempt ascent, or mock his sad exclusion from the doors of bliss.

Directly against this threshold, just under the blissful seat of Heaven, opened a wide passage from beneath, a passage down to Earth. As a shore bounds the sea, the wide opening marked the boundary of this universe. From the lowest tread that scaled the golden steps, Satan looked down with wonder at the sudden view of all this world at once. But envy more than wonder seized him at the sight, no small spectacle though measured against Heaven's example. From his vantage high above the spangled canopy, he surveyed all round from the eastern point of Libra to Aries; then from pole to pole he viewed in breath, and without further pause dove headlong in flight into the cosmic vacuum.

Between galaxies, over light years he sped, winding his way through the vast night, among numberless stars. Points of light they were in distant view, but passed close by seemed fully other worlds. But what or who dwelt there he made no pause to inquire, for his course was set by one where star gas mixed with angel light, the pure luminescence radiated by—and visible to—only spirits, as light perceives light, though removed far across Heaven's limitless plain or halfway across this finite universe. To his smart eye, that golden sentry, though small, burned like a torch in a sea of dimmer candles. Thus abused, the living beacon, fixed to guide to Earth all Heaven-sent missions, now led the fiend directly to his prey.

There he bent his course and landed straight upon the Sun's bright surface, that obscure landing spot perhaps yet undiscerned or charted by any astronomer's lens. Here the devil met new matter to gaze upon: terrain varied in radiant color and substance rare, but all alike imbued with blazing light, as glowing iron with fire. Part seemed gold, part garnet, ruby, or topaz—all flaming hot, yet cool compared to Hell's scorching climate—and where Hell burned black and gloomy, this place he found bright beyond expression. Undazzled, his eye commanded sight wide and far, for no obstacle interfered, nor fell there shade from any opaque body. The Sun's beams shot full as noon on Earth's equator, but upward here. The air too, nowhere so clear, sharpened his visual ray to objects far distant, whereby he soon discerned that glorious angel standing whose unique light, added to the Sun's, had guided him through all the myriad stars to this, as to a diamond in the sand. The angel's back was turned, but his brightness excelled undiminished. A crown of beaming sunny rays circled his head, beneath which, no less brilliant, fell golden locks waving round his winged shoulders. He seemed fixed in deep thought, while holding some great station.

The evil spirit, in hope to gain direction to the dwelling place of man, now contrived to change his shape, which otherwise might prompt some difficult questions from this guardian. Turning at the sound of Satan's approach, the bright angel saw no devil, but a cherub not yet come of age, in whose face youth smiled and to every limb diffused pure grace, so skillful was the fiend in fakery. He wore wings of many colored plume, sprinkled with gold, and held a silver wand, and under a jeweled band his flowing hair played about each red cheek. The counterfeit

cherub accosted the archangel Uriel, for he was im-
mediately known to Satan as one of the seven who
stand nearest God's throne, ready at command to
bear his swift errands all through Heaven and, as
now apparent, down to Earth as well:

"Greetings, bright Uriel, honored watchman of
Heaven and this new world. Intense desire to see
and know all these new wondrous works of the
Creator, but chiefly man, for whom all was created,
has brought me from the choirs of cherubim thus
wandering alone. Brightest seraph, tell me, if no
restriction forbids, in which of all these shining orbs
has man his home, that I may find him, and with
secret gaze or open admiration, behold him on whom
the Maker has bestowed a world."

So spoke the hypocrite unperceived, for neither
man nor angel can discern hypocrisy—the only evil
that walks invisible through Heaven and Earth
except to God alone. And often, though wisdom
be awake, suspicion sleeps at wisdom's gate, and
goodness thinks no ill where no ill seems. So now
Uriel, though regent of the Sun and held sharpest-
sighted spirit of all in Heaven, was deceived, and
through his own uprightness thus complied with the
fraudulent request:

"Fair angel, blessed is the eagerness which leads
you here alone to witness with your eyes what some,
content with reports, hear of only in Heaven. Won-
derful indeed are all God's works to know and to
be had in remembrance always with delight. What
created mind can comprehend their number or the
infinite wisdom that brought them forth? I was one
who saw when, at his word, the formless mass, this
world's material mold, came to a heap; confusion

heard his voice and wild uproar stood ruled, vast infinitude confined, till, at his second bidding, darkness fled, light shined, and order from disorder sprung. The stable elements of earth, flood, air, and fire hastened then swiftly to their several quarters, and this ethereal quintessence floated upward, gaseous with various moving forms that swirled and exploded and condensed into these numberless stars you see, each given his appointed place, each his course.

"Look downward on that globe which shines with borrowed light sent from here. That place is Earth, seat of man; that light his day, without which, night would invade there as it does the other hemisphere. That spot to which I point is Paradise, Adam's abode; those lofty shades, his bower. Proceed—the way you cannot miss—and fill your desire which seeks to know the work of God. Then return to Heaven with yet higher praise for him, Creator of all wonders."

Satan bowed low, as is customary in Heaven, where none neglects due honor and reverence to superior angels, then took his leave and dove steep down toward the coast of Earth, his journey's end and our beginning woe.

VIII

The Garden of Eden

OH, that some warning voice had cried out in Paradise while still there was time to alert our first parents of the approach of their unknown enemy, that they might have escaped his mortal snare! For now Satan stood freshly alighted atop Niphates, the Assyrian mount overlooking Eden, where soon he would wreak on innocent frail man his rage at the loss of that first war in Heaven. Yet no eagerness prompted him to begin the dire attempt; rather, horror and doubt boiled within his tumultuous breast, distracting his troubled thoughts. From the bottom stirred the Hell within him, for he could fly from Hell no more than he could fly from himself, but brought it within him and round about him, it's horror undiminished by change of place. Now conscience woke despair and bitter memory of what he had been, what he had become, and what worse must be, as from worse deeds worse sufferings must ensue.

Towards Eden, which lay in pleasant prospect, he fixed his grieved look. Before him lay all the splendor of the valley's abundant greenery: the lush Primordial forest, sweet in luxuriant growth, recent offspring to this fertile Earth. Here youthful nature played at will her virgin fancies, above rule, pouring forth wilderness, or spreading her flaxen savanna in roaming bands, broad and placid. And above, the paternal virtue of the full-blazing Sun shone, newly revealed. So wondrously was set his station bright, to gently warm the entire Earth, and to each inward part, with gentle penetration, shoot invisible seeds of life, even to the deep. To him set high in his zenith, Satan turned his passion:

"You who look down from your unique dominion over this new world like a god, crowned with surpassing glory, at whose sight all the stars hide their diminished heads, to you I call with no friendly voice to tell you how I hate your beams that bring to memory the state from which I fell, more glorious than yours, where pride and ambition threw me down, warring in Heaven against a matchless King —though he deserved no such enmity from me, for he made me what I was in my exalted place, and in his good reproached no one. Nor was his service hard. What could be less to ask than to afford him praise and pay him thanks? Yet all his good proved ill to me and wrought only malice. Lifted up so high, I disdained subjection, and thinking one step higher would set me highest, in a moment quit the immense debt of endless gratitude so burdensome—always paying, always owing. I could not then see that a grateful mind, aware of its debt, pays with its awareness and owes no more. What burden then remains?

"If only he had ordained me some inferior angel, then might I have remained happy. Then perhaps no unbounded hope would have raised vain ambition. Still, some other power as great might have aspired and drawn me to his part. Yet other great powers did not fall to that temptation, but stood unshaken from within or from without. Had not I the same free will and power to stand? Who or what have I then to accuse but Heaven's free love, dealt equally to all? Accursed be his love then! Since love or hate to me alike deal eternal woe. Nay, cursed be my own miserable will, since it chose freely against his what it now so justly regrets.

"Ah, misery! Which way shall I fly? All is infinite wrath and infinite despair. Whichever way I fly is Hell. I myself am Hell. In the lowest deep a lower deep still threatening to devour me opens wide, to which the Hell I suffer seems a Heaven. Then must I relent at last? Is there no place left for repentance, nor for pardon, except by submission?—that word which fills me with contempt and dread of shame among my compatriots below, which I seduced with promises and boasts that I could subdue the Omnipotent. Little they know how weakly I now endure that boast so vain, or under what torments inwardly I groan while they adore me on the throne of Hell. Still lower do I fall, though high advanced with crown and scepter, supreme only in misery. Such joy is found by ambition.

Paradise Lost

"But say I could repent and by act of grace obtain my former state, how soon would that high place recall high thoughts? Suppose he should relent and again bestow grace to all, on our promise of renewed submission. Should we then celebrate his throne with forced hymns and strained hallelujahs, while he sits lordly and envied, his altar breathing the sweet flowery fragrance of our servile offerings, our new task in Heaven—a wearisome eternity spent in worship paid to him we hate. How soon would falsely sworn submission be withdrawn and vows made in pain and coercion be renounced, made void in that state of ease? Would not all lead to a worse relapse and heavier fall? The purchase price would be dear for but a short reconcilement. Knowing this as he must, my punisher is as far from granting peace as am I from begging it. Where wounds of deadly hate have pierced so deep, all hope is excluded. Behold, instead he creates for his new delight Mankind, to take our place, and for it, this new world. So, farewell hope, and with hope, fear and remorse as well. All good to me is lost. Evil must become my good. For in evil at least I hold divided empire with Heaven's King, and will reign perhaps even the greater part, as man and his new world may soon know."

As he spoke, each passion dimmed his face; anger, envy, and despair marred his borrowed visage and betrayed his falseness to any watching eye, for heavenly minds are ever clear from such foul temperament. Suddenly aware of this, he fully smoothed his brow, supplanting his mad demeanor with outward calm, and was the first to practice concealed malice under saintly show; then down the mount and across the open plain he fared.

Near the border of Eden there rose into view a green plateau that crowned a steep wilderness mound, whose sides, overgrown with thicket, denied all passage. Up the mound, branching palm, cedar, stately pine, and fir of insuperable height and loftiest shade ascended in majestic ranks, shade above shade. Yet higher than their tops rose the vine-covered wall of Paradise. From that delicious enclosure gentle breezes fanned down odors of spice and native perfumes pure enough to drive all sadness but despair. Those sweet unwary scents welcomed their murderer, who, pensive and slow, approached on foot the steep ascent. But the wild hill was so thickly entwined with tangled underbrush as to prevent all access for man or beast. There was one gate only, which faced east on the other side and stood locked secure. In contempt of all this, the archfiend high overleapt with one bound all obstruction of hill and thicket and wall, and with steep drop lighted on his feet within—as a prowling wolf driven by hunger, who overconfidently leaps the fence into the field where shepherds watch. Once inside, up he flew into the Tree of Life, the middle tree and highest that grew there, where he sat unaware of the power and virtue of that life-giving plant of immortality, using it only as a place of vantage, there to devise death to those that lived. (So little do any but God alone know to value the good before them and instead pervert the best of things to worst abuse.) Beneath him now, exposed to all the delights of human senses, Satan viewed with new wonder in this single place nature's whole wealth, a Heaven on Earth. Out of the ground all around grew trees of noblest kind for sight, smell, or taste—trees laden with fairest fruit and blossoms of bright rainbow colors on which the glad Sun mixed his golden hue. Amid them all, the Tree of Life bloomed ambrosial fruit of living gold; and next to life, our death, the Tree of Knowledge, grew.

Southward through Eden flowed a large river upon which sat the garden Paradise. Its course was not deflected by the mountain, but engulfed and swallowed underneath. Through veins of porous earth, its water was drawn up with natural thirst to a fresh fountain spring at the highest part, and with many a bubbly brook and stream the whole garden was fed. The waters meandered and rippled over pearly rocks and sands of gold under hanging branches, to visit each plant and flower of Paradise, both where the morning Sun first warmed the open field and where unpierced shade enveloped the bowers even at noontide. Between rich delicious groves were interposed level grassy expanses, where flocks grazed the tender herb. Here sat a palmy hillock; there the lap of some watered valley, spreading her store of flowers in every hue. These grew not in fastidious, carefully planted beds, but poured forth in nature's profuse bounty. On another side, shady grottoes of cool recess were cloaked with gently creeping vines luxuriant with purple grape and rose without thorn. Murmuring waters cascaded down the hills' diverging slopes, or united their streams in a lake that held her crystal mirror to the leafy fringed bank. Birds added their choir to harmonize with leaves dancing in the breeze in celebration of the Assyrian garden's eternal season of spring.

The Garden of Eden

All this delight lay before the undelighted fiend. Without sympathy he scrutinized all the living creatures new and strange, till among them he discovered two of far nobler shape, erect and tall, godlike in naked majesty, the seeming worthy lords of all. In their looks the divine image of their glorious Maker shone, though differently in each. He seemed formed for contemplation and for valor; she for softness and sweet attractive grace. His fair large brow and noble eye declared absolute rule. At the top of his forehead his umber locks parted and hung clustering almost to his wide shoulders. She wore as a veil down to her slender waist her unadorned golden tresses, which fell forward in disheveled waves as she moved and with gentle sway of her head rolled back. Secret parts were not then concealed by unchaste guilt or sin-bred shame of nature's works. Naked, they shunned not each other's sight, nor sight of God, nor angel—for they thought no ill. Hand in hand they passed, the loveliest pair that ever since embraced God's love or each other's: Adam, goodliest of men since born of his sons, and Eve, fairest of her daughters.

The two sat themselves down by a fresh stream bed, under a tuft of whispering shade, having toiled at their pleasant gardening labor no more than sufficed to make rest more comforting and wholesome thirst and appetite more gratifying to appease. The nearby boughs yielded them their supper fruits, nectarine and peach, as they reclined on the soft downy bank patterned with flowers. Between gentle conversation and endearing smiles they chewed the savory pulp and with the rind scooped cool drink from the brimming stream. About them played the frisky beasts that have since become wild, avoiding man and each other. The sporting lion reared and fondled the lamb with his paw, making them laugh. The fox and the leopard gamboled before them without quarrel. Others, having fed, sat gazing or reclined and chewed their cud, for the Sun's decline was hastening now, and in the east waking stars began to spangle the gray sky. Here beheld was man in his happiest life, in simplicity and spotless innocence.

Satan gazed upon the sylvan scene. With grief his eyes appraised these creatures advanced into his former place of favor—creatures of different mold, Earth-born, not spirits, yet little inferior in divine resemblance, such grace was poured on their shape by the hand that formed them. How little the gentle pair thought what change approached, or soon how all those delights would vanish and deliver them to woe, more miserable then, the more their taste was now of joy. Their high and happy seat seemed poorly secured by Heaven to keep out such a foe as now was entered.

Yet his malice was not directed at them, whom he could pity for their impending doom, though he remain unpitied. "No, it is only friendship and close alliance I seek with you," he whispered, "so close that I must dwell with you, or you with me. My dwelling may not please your senses as this fair Paradise, but as such you must accept your Master's work. He gave it to me, and I as freely give it to you. Hell shall unfold her widest gates and send forth all her kings to welcome you two lords of Earth. There will be ample room, more than these narrow limits, to receive all your children. If the change displeases you, thank him who puts me to this unwelcome chore of revenge on you who have done me no ill."

Lest he should soften at their harmless innocence, as he was perhaps inclined, duty to his empire, enlarged with revenge, must override disgrace and compel him now to do what otherwise, though damned to eternity, he should abhor. So the fiend excused his devilish deeds with necessity, the tyrant's plea. He descended from his lofty perch on that high tree and alighted among the four-footed herd, himself now one of them, then another, changing at will to the shape that best served his end, to nearer view his prey undetected and learn what more he might of their state, revealed by words or actions. Now a lion, round about them he stalked with fiery glare; now a tiger, as by chance might spy in some forest two gentle fawns at play, he crouched close, then rising, moved to another position—as if seeking the best ground from which to rush and seize them both, gripping one in each paw—when the sound of new utterance turned him all ear, as speech flowed from Adam, first of men, to Eve, first of women:

"Eve, sole partner of all these joys, dearer than all, witness the infinite good in the Power that made us, that raised us from the dust and placed us here in all this happiness. He is as generous as he is infinite, for of all this kindness he gains nothing for himself, he who has no need, and asks of us no other service than to keep this one, this easy charge: that of all the trees in Paradise that bear delicious fruit so varied, only the Tree of Knowledge, planted by the Tree of Life, is that from which we are to abstain and not taste. So near grows Death to Life—whatever death is, some dreadful thing, no doubt—for well you know God has pronounced it death to taste that tree. This is the only sign of our obedience required among so many signs of power and rule which he has bestowed upon us, giving us dominion over all other creatures that possess earth, air, and sea. We shall not think harsh or difficult one easy prohibition, when to all other things we enjoy free access with unlimited choice of manifold delights, but shall ever praise him and extol his bounty as we follow our pleasant task to prune these growing plants and tend these flowers—a task which, even were it toilsome, with you would turn pure delight."

"My love," came Eve's reply, "for whom and from whom I was formed, flesh of your flesh, and without whom I have no purpose, we owe to him all praises and daily thanks, I especially, who enjoy so much the happier lot in that I have you, so much my superior in all ways, while you can nowhere find a companion equal to yourself, whose manly grace and wisdom excel all beauty."

With adoring eyes and meek surrender, half-embracing, she leaned on our first father. Half her swelling breast met his, bare under her gold flowing tresses. Adam smiled on her beauty and submissive charms, and with his lips pressed hers so pure, which paused, then yielded with sweet, reluctant, amorous delay.

"Hateful, tormenting sight!" The demon turned away, eyeing them askance with a malign, jealous leer. "These two enjoy their fill of bliss, enraptured in one another's arms, while I am thrust to Hell with neither joy nor love, but fierce desire unfulfilled not the least among my torments. But let me not forget what I have learned from their own mouths. All is not theirs, it seems. One fatal tree there stands called *Knowledge*, forbidden them to taste. Knowledge forbidden? Senseless. Suspicious. Why should their Lord deny them that? Can it be sin to know? Can it be death? And is it only by ignorance that they possess their happy state? Or is it merely a test of their obedience and their faith? Either way, it proves a fair foundation on which to stage their ruin. The way then is clear. I will excite their minds with desire to know more and to reject selfish commands designed to keep them low and deny them knowledge that might exalt them equal with gods. Aspiring to be such, they will taste and die. Live while yet you may, happy pair. Enjoy your brief pleasures, for long woes are to follow."

Scornfully he left them and set out to explore the garden and pick the best time and place and manner in which to execute his plan. Meanwhile, far to the west, where sky meets earth and ocean, the setting Sun aimed his evening rays eastward against the gate of Paradise. The entrance way fell between rocks of alabaster piled toward the clouds, widely visible, with one winding ascent accessible from Eden's plain. The rest was craggy cliff that further overhung the more it rose, impossible to climb. Between these rocky pillars, awaiting night, sat Gabriel, chief of the angelic guard, charged to watch that no evil thing approach or enter this happy place. Near at hand hung celestial armor, shields, helmets, and spears, flaming with diamonds and gold. Around him Heaven's unarmed youths exercised in sporting games, when from the sky, gliding down through the evening mist on a sunbeam, rode the bright archangel Uriel, swift as a shooting star. Landing before his allies, he began in haste:

"Gabriel, this day at high noon an Earthbound spirit came to halt at my post. He seemed eager to know more of the Almighty's work, and chiefly of man. I directed his way, which he resumed bent on all speed. My eye pursued his descent. He lighted on the mount that lies north of Eden, where I discerned his manner to be alien from Heaven. His actions betrayed foul passions, and his countenance was disfigured more than could befall a benevolent spirit. I pursued him, but lost sight of him in the shade. One of the banished crew, I fear, has ventured from the deep to raise new troubles."

"No creature has passed this gate but those who come well-known from Heaven," returned the imperial sentinel, "and none since noon this day. But if a spirit of another sort is minded to overleap these earthly bounds, these physical walls will not prevent him. If he whom you describe lurks within the circuit of these walks, in whatever shape, by dawn tomorrow I shall know."

Uriel returned to his charge on that bright beam, whose point, now raised higher by temporal degrees, bore him slope downward toward the Sun, which had fallen beneath the Azores. Clad in reflected purple and gold he went, as evening covered all else in her sober cloak of twilight gray. Silence accompanied each beast and bird to his grassy bed or high nest, all but the wakeful nightingale, who all night sang his amorous melody. The heavens glowed with living sapphires. Hesperus, the brightest, led the starry host, till the moon, rising in clouded majesty, unveiled her peerless light and threw her silver mantle over the darkness, as Adam reluctantly terminated sweet discourse with his spouse:

"Fair Eve, the hour of night weighs our eyelids with the soft dew of sleep. Tomorrow, before fresh morning streaks the east with its first approach of light, we must be risen and at our pleasant labor, if we are to keep pace with these flowery arbors and green alleys that mock our scant cultivation with overgrown branches and ever-falling blossoms."

"My perfect partner," happily she answered, "conversing with you, I forget all time; all hours are equally pleasing, first breath of dewy morn or silent advance of glittering starlight, as now in view—this glorious sight, which makes me wonder for whom these gems of heaven shine all night long, when sleep has shut all eyes."

"They have their course to finish," said Adam, "round the Earth by tomorrow's evening. From land to land, through nations yet unborn, they set and rise, lest total darkness by night regain her old possession and extinguish life in nature and all things. These soft fires warm and nourish, with gentle heat, all life that grows on Earth, and condition it to receive perfection from the Sun's more potent ray.

"Though unveiled in the deep of night, Heaven's glory does not lack spectators. A thousand spiritual creatures walk the Earth unseen, both when we wake and when we sleep. All these behold God's works with ceaseless praise. How often have we heard echoes of celestial voices in the midnight air? Their blissful songs permeate the night and lift our thoughts to Heaven."

Paradise Lost

So Eve and Adam retired to their bedchamber, the place chosen for them by the Creator when he framed all things to man's pleasurable use. For thickest protection, the roof was woven in shade laurel and myrtle and other firm and fragrant leaf. In either side, acanthus and varied bushy shrub fenced up the green wall. Roses and jasmine and iris of all hue reared high their heads in between like a mosaic. Underfoot, inlay of violet, crocus, and hyacinth embroidered the ground, more rich and colorful than the costliest carpet. No other creature, neither bird, nor beast, nor insect dared enter here, such was their awe of man. In this sequestered bower had the espoused Eve first decked her nuptial bed with flowers, garlands, and sweet-smelling herbs, as heavenly choirs sang the marriage song, in that day the Creator first brought her to our forefather.

Now, before the bower entrance, under the open sky, both stood and in these words adored the God that made sky, air, earth and heaven, all which they beheld by the moon's resplendent globe and starry cape:

"Maker of the night and of the day in which we have finished our appointed work, happy in our mutual help and love, the crown of all our joy ordained by thee, in this place of abundance for us too large we await a race, promised by thee, that shall extol with us thy infinite goodness, both when we wake and when we seek, as now, thy gift of sleep."

This prayer said as two in one mind, hand in hand they went into their shady recess, and with no need to put off such troublesome disguises as we wear, directly lay side by side. Nor did Adam turn from his fair spouse, nor Eve refuse the rites of conjugal love. Soon, lulled by nightingales, they slept, embracing, as on their naked limbs the flowery roof showered patterned shades of roses.

Hail, wedded love! Mysterious, exclusive, ordained source of human life! Here Love expends his golden shafts and lights his constant lamp. Heed not those hypocrites who austerely talk of abstinence in Paradise, defaming what God declares pure. For our Maker bid increase and multiply; who bid abstain then, but our destroyer, foe to God and man?

†

Night had measured half her shadowy course across the moonlit landscape when from their ivory gate the cherubim came forth at the accustomed hour, armed to their night watches. He whose tall silhouette bespoke high command issued instruction to his next in rank:

"Azziel, draw off half of these and coast the south with strictest watch, while the others wheel with me the north; our circuit meets full west."

They parted as a flame—half turning left, half to the right. From each half one strong and trusty spirit was called and these two given their charge:

"Ithuriel and Zephon, with winged speed search through the interior of this garden. Leave no nook uncovered, but especially where those two fair creatures lodge, now laid asleep, suspecting no harm. This evening at sundown, report came of some infernal spirit observed Earthward bent—one escaped from the bars of Hell, on evil errand no doubt. Should you find him, seize and bring him to me at the western end."

Paradise Lost

So saying, Gabriel led on his radiant files, out-shining the moon, as the two he had charged moved to the interior in search of the intruder. Directly to the bower they headed first to secure the safety of the sleeping pair. There they found the one they sought, squat like a toad, close at the ear of sleeping Eve, testing his devilish skills to reach the organs of her fancy. Intent he was to taint pure sleep with forged illusions, phantasms, and dreams that inspire discontented thoughts, vain hopes, inordinate desires.

Thus occupied, he was oblivious to their approach, till Ithuriel touched him lightly with his spear. Up he started, inflaming the air like a heap of black gunpowder touched by a spark. The two stepped back, amazed so suddenly to behold the grisly king, but quickly recovered and unmoved with fear, accosted him:

"Which of those rebel spirits adjudged to Hell, now escaped, are you?" asked the one, and the other quickly following: "Why do you sit like an enemy in wait here watching at the head of these that sleep?"

"Do you not know me?" asked Satan, full of scorn. "Not to know me argues yourselves unknown, the lowest of your throng."

To which Zephon replied, answering scorn with scorn: "You err to think your shape unchanged from when you stood among those upright and pure in Heaven. With your place lost, that glory also departed, and you now match your sin and place of doom in looks obscure and foul. But come, for you shall give account, be sure, if not to us, to him who sent us, whose charge is to keep this place inviolate and these from harm."

The Garden of Eden

The devil stood abashed before the cherub's grave rebuke, severe in youthful beauty, and felt how awful goodness is, and saw virtue in her shape how graceful, and grieved his loss, most of all that they could see visible degeneration in his aspect.

"Lead on," he snapped. "If I must contend, let it be with the sender, not the sent."

"Your choice saves me proving what a single upright servant can do against one high in evil, since evil is weak however high," said Zephon.

The fiend gave no reply, overcome with rage, but like a proud steed in reins, went haughtily on. He saw it vain to flee. As they drew near the western point where the circling squadrons had just met, peering from the front, Gabriel discerned Ithuriel and Zephon through the shade, and with them a third of regal bearing. The two approached and in brief related of whom they brought and where found.

"Satan, why have you broken the bounds imposed by your transgressions?" asked Gabriel, who well knew the prisoner. (His two captors were agape to learn they had caught none but the prince of Hell.) "Think you to boldly enter this place unimpeded, intent to violate the sleep of those whose safety God has planted in our charge?"

With contemptuous brow, Satan answered: "You were esteemed wise in Heaven, Gabriel, and such I regarded you, but this query puts me to doubt. Lives there one who loves his pain, or who would not, finding way, break loose from Hell, whatever cause places him there? You would yourself, no doubt, and boldly venture to whatever place is farthest from pain, as I have sought shelter in this place. Let him who imprisons us bar his iron gates more sure if he intends our stay in that dark dungeon. So much for your question; the rest is true: they found me where they say, but that does not imply violence or harm."

"Heaven has lost one profound judge of wisdom, who judges it improper for me to question his invasion, but wise for him to fly from punishment pronounced by God." Gabriel mocked him. "What pain can be worse than infinite wrath provoked, such as your flight shall incur? But how is it you flee alone? Why has not all Hell broke loose with you? Is pain to them less evil, or are you less hardy to endure it then they?"

"Well you know that I shrink not from pain," he returned, "as witnessed when I withstood your fiercest blows in battle, which proved not fierce enough, till aided by the Almighty's blasting thunder. But still you accuse with words that expose your inexperience in what it is that a faithful leader must do. He does not place all his men in risk through ways of danger he has not himself tried. Thereby, I alone first undertook to wing the desolate abyss and seek this newly created world, in hope to find a better abode in which to settle my afflicted armies."

"First, wise to fly pain; next, the brave scout," said Gabriel. "Your contradictions argue no leader, but a marked liar. And to the title 'leader' dare you add 'faithful'? Sacred name profaned! Faithful to whom? To your rebellious crew?—army of fiends, fit body to fit head. Sly hypocrite, pretended patron of liberty, who would dispossess Heaven's Supreme Monarch but to glorify yourself! Now heed this warning: If you are not departed from these sacred limits within the hour, I alone will drag you back in chains to the infernal pit and see that you think hard before venturing loose again."

Then Satan's rage waxed hot. He stood like a defiant mountain. "When I am your captive, talk then of chains, proud servant, fit only to draw under yoke your master's chariot. Till then far heavier load expect to bear from my prevailing arm."

As he spoke, the angelic squadron slowly bent to hem him in with tilted spears, thick as a field of waving wheat. Now dreadful conflict might have ensued, disturbing not only Paradise, but all the elements with its fury, had not the Almighty intervened with his fateful sign put forth in Heaven's constellations, upon seeing which, Gabriel warned the fiend:

"I know your strength, Satan, and you see mine before you, neither our own, but each given from above. What folly then to boast what arms can do, since yours can do no more than Heaven permits, nor mine, though outnumbering you here enough to trample you like mud. If you need proof, look up and read your weakness in the celestial sign where you are weighed and your doom foretold if you resist."

The fiend looked up and knew his futile plight. Counterpoised above in Libra's scales hung the consequences of parting against those of fight. Of these two, the latter quick upflew, outweighed, and kicked the beam, signifying his defeat. Wasting no more words, the intruder fled, muttering, and with him the shades of night.

The Visitation

SOON morning advanced her rosy steps through
Eden on the eastern side and bathed the Earth with
pearly glow. So airy light was Adam's sleep, bred
of pure digestion and climate so temperate, that the
mere sound of rippling brook, or leaves fanned by
the dawn breeze, or the morning song of birds in
the trees was enough to stir him and his mate. So
much more was his wonder upon waking to find
Eve inanimate, her hair disheveled, and with a look
of unquiet rest. He leaned on his side, half-raised,
and touching her hand, whispered:

"Awake, Eve. The morning shines and the fresh
field calls us. See how nature blooms ever new and
paints her colors fresh. Let us be up before the prime
of morning passes."

She woke but with a start and seeing her husband,
embraced him quickly, trembling. "Oh Adam, so

glad am I to see your perfect face and the return of morning. Never have I passed such a night as this or dreamed such dreams—if dreams they were. Such distress my mind has never known before. In the night I thought I heard a soft voice close at my ear, calling me forth to walk; at first I thought it yours. 'Why sleep now, Eve?' it asked. 'Now is the pleasant time, the cool, the silence which yields only to the sweet love songs of night-warbling birds. The moon reigns full and sets off the scene with more pleasing light than day—all in vain if no one comes to see. Heaven wakes with all his eyes to look upon none but you, nature's desire. In your sight, all things find joy to gaze with ravishment upon your beauty.'

"I rose to heed your call, but found you not there. I went to find you and it seemed I came before the tree called Knowledge. More appealing it looked, much more than by day. And as I stood before it, I became aware of another beside me, one winged as those from Heaven, often seen by us. His dewy locks distilled sweet perfume as he also gazed upon the tree and spoke:

"'Oh fruited plant, filled to excess, no one thinks to ease your load and taste your sweets, neither god nor man. Is knowledge so despised? Or is it envy that places this restriction? Let him forbid who will; no one shall longer withhold from me your offered good.'

"Then without hesitation he reached forth and tasted. I felt a deep chill of horror at such bold words, backed by the deed. But he spoke again, seemingly overjoyed:

"'Oh sweet divine fruit, much sweeter because forbidden as only fit for gods, yet able to make gods of men. And why not gods of men, since to have divine knowledge of good is to make goodness grow yet more abundant? Here, happy Eve, you partake also. Happy though you are, yet happier can you be. Taste this and be among the gods, yourself a goddess, no longer confined to Earth. Ascend to Heaven with me and see what life gods live there.'

"Then he drew near and held to me—even to my mouth—that same fruit which he had tasted. The pleasant savory smell so quickened my appetite that I felt I could not resist but taste. Immediately, up to the clouds with him I flew and beheld the immense Earth outstretched beneath in wide, spectacular view. I floated, amazed at this change and godlike flight, when suddenly my guide was gone, and I seemed to sink back down into sleep. How glad I am to wake and find this but a dream!"

"Poor Eve, pure Eve, the trouble of your thoughts this night affects me equally," said Adam, aching at her distress. "I fear this dream springs from some unknown evil, I know not where, only that you are not its source. But in the soul, when nature rests, reason also retires into her private cell, and in her absence imagination sometimes wakes to imitate her, often producing wild work, with misjointed thoughts and memories and notions half-formed. I think I see in your dreams some such resemblance of our last evening's talk, with some strange additions. But do not fret; evil may come and go into the mind of God or men and leave no spot or blame behind. I read in this more hope than harm, that what in sleep you did abhor to dream, waking you never will consent to do. Now where are those looks cheerful and serene that I am accustomed to see smile upon the world each morning?"

His gentle words revived her, and he kissed a tear that stood ready to fall from her eye, the gracious sign of her sweet remorse and pious awe that feared to have offended. As they came forth from under their green roof, the Sun shot his red ray parallel to the Earth, illuminating all the east of Paradise and Eden's wide plain. They bowed low and began their morning prayers, praise sent to their Maker, as it was, in new and varied style each dawn:

> *Thou Sun, of this Great World both Eye and Soul,*
> *Fairest of stars, last in the train of Night,*
> *Sure pledge of Day, that crown'st the smiling morn,*
> *Chief of his glorious works, acknowledge him,*
> *Parent of Good, thy greater; sound his praise*
> *In thy eternal course, both when thou climb'st*
> *And when high Noon has gained, and when thou fall'st;*
> *Wander thy mystic circle in warm dance,*
> *And let thy fires that nourish us extol*
> *His might, who out of Darkness called up Light.*
> *Almighty, thine is Goodness beyond thought.*
> *Hail, universal Lord, be bounteous still,*
> *While day arises, that sweet hour of prime,*
> *To give us only Good, and if the night*
> *Has gathered aught of evil to conceal,*
> *Disperse it now as Light dispels the Dark.*

The Visitation

They prayed, innocent, and soon recovering peace and calm to their thoughts, went on to their pleasant gardening work among sweet dews and flowers, where branches of fruit trees overreached too far and needed trim, or where the wandering vine sought guidance up the fruitless oak to adorn his barren leaves. Thus employed in their tasks were they beheld with love and pity from above, where a gentle spirit, chosen for his friendly nature, was summoned to carry out an earthly mission.

"Raphael," said Heaven's high King, "You have heard what stir on Earth has been raised in Paradise by Satan, and how he has this night disturbed the human pair, attempting through them to ruin all mankind. Go therefore this midday and find in what bower or shade Adam retires from the heat of noon, and there converse with him, friend to friend. Advise him that his happy condition rests in his own power, left to his own free will. Warn him not to be overconfident in this freedom. Tell him of his danger and what enemy is now plotting against him and his wife, not by violence, from which they are protected, but by deceit and lies, to bring them down to his own fallen state. Let them know this lest, willfully transgressing, they plead they were unprepared or unforewarned."

So the Eternal Father fulfilled all justice. Without delay the winged saint flew through the midst of Heaven straight away to Heaven's gate, which gave way to his speed, parting on each hand, and opened wide, self-propelled on golden hinges. From here, unobstructed by cloud or star, he saw by power of celestial sight, though tiny yet distinct from other shining globes, the Earth, crowned with the Garden of God. Down he sailed, prone in flight, through the vast ethereal sky, between worlds, on steady wing. Soon he was gliding the polar winds, till, within the realm of soaring eagles, he fanned the yielding air to break his lightning descent with splendorous wing-spread, gilded by the rays of the Sun, and seemed to all the gazing fowl a phoenix. Lighting on the eastern cliff of Paradise, he resumed his manlike stature, a graceful seraph. His wings hung from each broad shoulder in regal ornament like a cloak of downy gold. A starry belt girded his waist, and his loins and thighs were skirted with reflective gold and colors dipped in Heaven's light. Like Mercury, messenger of gods, he stood and shook his plumes, filling the noon air with ambrosial fragrance.

The bands of angels under watch quickly recognized him and rose in honor of his high rank, guessing him bound on some important mission. He passed their glittering tents and came into the field of bliss, passing through groves of myrrh and flowering odors of cinnamon and balm. His approach through the spicy forest was discerned by Adam, who sat in the door of his cool bower, shaded from the fervid rays of the noon Sun, now mounted high to warm Earth's inmost womb. Within, Eve was preparing savory fruits and nectareous drink from grapes and berries to satisfy the hungry hour, when Adam called to her:

"Come quickly, Eve, and see what glorious sight moves this way from among those eastward trees. It is as if another sun has risen on midnoon. A spirit set upon some mysterious quest deigns to cross our garden on his way, or perhaps he brings some great message from Heaven and will consent to be our guest this day. Go and bring forth with abundance what your stores contain fit to honor and receive this heavenly stranger. Well may we afford our givers their own gifts."

"Little is stored where so much hangs on the stalk ripe for use in all seasons," replied Eve, "but I will hurry and collect the choicest pick from each branch, enough to entertain our guest and show how God has spread his bounties here on Earth as in Heaven." And she set about her task to choose what delicacies best would serve in pleasing combination. From each tender stalk she gathered fruit of rough or smooth rind, or bearded husk, or shell. Wide choice was hers, for what rare succulent delights Mother Earth today yields to us in these West Indies or Polynesian isles, in Asia or the Mediterranean shore—all this once in a single garden grew. These luxuries she brought to table in their most enhancing mix, heaped with unsparing hand. For drink, wine and liquors she crushed and blended with expert skill, and smooth creams pressed from sweet kernels. These she poured into delicate clay vessels she had fashioned. Lastly, the ground she strewed with roses and scented leaves.

Meanwhile, Adam went forth to greet his godlike guest: the prince of Earth to meet a prince of Heaven, accompanied with no more train than his own complete perfection, more regal and solemn in his nakedness than all the tedious pomp and longled procession that attend the court of rich kings. Nearing his presence, Adam bowed and spoke, not in awe, yet with meek reverence to the spirit's visibly superior nature:

"Visitor from Heaven—for no other place can produce such glory—since you condescend to forsake awhile that happy place and honor this, come rest with us in our shady bower and sit and taste what choicest fruit this garden bears, till this meridian heat is over and the Sun more cool declines."

Said the noble emissary: "Adam, you and your place of dwelling have not been created less than pleasing and inviting, even to spirits of Heaven. Lead on then to the cool of your bower, for I am free to share your company till evening."

A mound of grassy turf formed the table, with mossy seats round, and amply piled from side to side. The arbor was decked with florets and fragrant smells, while Eve stood unadorned except in her own loveliness, unstained virtue her only veil. At the entrance the angelic traveler bestowed his salutation:

"Hail, mother of mankind! whose fruitful womb shall fill the world more numerous with sons than the plentiful fruits heaped on this table by the trees of God."

"The Earth yields to us these bounties for our food and our delight," she replied, "but perhaps unsavory to spiritual tastes. Only this I know: one Celestial Father gives to all."

"Therefore, what he gives to man," answered the friendly angel, "who is in part spiritual, will not be found inferior by purest spirits. Their ethereal substance requires food as does your more tangible, for whatever is created needs to be sustained and fed. In Heaven the trees bear ambrosial fruit, the vines yield nectar, and from the boughs each morning drop dews of honey. Yet here God has varied his bounty with new delights to compare with Heaven's, and I think I shall not hesitate to partake."

The Visitation

So down they sat. Eve crowned their cups with pleasing liquors, and they commenced to dine—the angel with taste as keen and hunger no less real than that of the human couple. When they had had their fill of food and drink, it came to Adam's mind not to let the occasion pass given him by this great encounter to know of things above his world, so he carefully framed his speech to draw forth the honored guest:

"Heavenly minister, you have shown your kind regard in this honor done to man. Under his lowly roof have you entered and tasted these earthly fruits, not food of angels, yet accepted as such, seemingly as willingly as if you had been at one of Heaven's high feasts. Yet how can such compare?"

"Adam, one Almighty exists," said Raphael, "from whom all things proceed and up to him return, if not depraved from good. Such is the perfection in all he created. All is of one matter, endowed with various forms and various degrees of substance, and things that live, with life. Each strives upward to become more refined, more spiritual and pure, as from the root springs lighter the green stalk; from this the leaves more airy; and last, the bright consummate flower, breathing fragrant spirits. So flowers and their fruits give nourishment to man by gradual scale, feeding first the vital, then the intellectual, giving both life and sense, imagination and understanding, from which the soul receives reason; and reason is its being. So do not wonder if I do not refuse what God saw good for you, for I too convert it, as do you, to my own proper substance. Time may come when men may feast with angels and find that diet not incompatible. And from those special nutriments your bodies may at last turn all to spirit, and winged, ascend the air as we, or dwell at choice here or in heavenly paradises."

They rose, and Adam accompanied his guest outside to walk in the garden while Eve remained behind to tend the bower. Not that their discourse would have delighted her less, nor was she less capable than her husband to hear such matters high, but she willingly reserved that pleasure, knowing Adam would later, in their solitude, relate to her all that was said, adding pleasing digressions and inter-mixing high debate with sweet caresses, as from his lips more than words would please her.

"Spirit," Adam commenced, "how wonderfully you teach us the set way of nature and the scale of created things, in which, through meditation, by steps we may ascend to God. But say, do not heavenly spirits also love, and how do they express their love: by looks only, or in immediate touch as we?"

The angel answered with a rosy smile, "What joy is expressed through your body, we radiate through-out our pure essence. When spirits embrace, their mix is total, as air with air. No physical obstacle of limbs or membrane or flesh limits the union of pure with pure. But let it suffice that you know we are happy—and without love, no happiness can be."

"Through marriage I have perceived this truth," said Adam, "for though I find such delight in all things here of taste and sight and smell, these deli-cacies work no vehement desire, but in the woman's presence I become transported. There I first felt pas-sion and strange disturbance. While in all other enjoyments I was able to remain superior and un-moved, here only I grew weak under the charm of beauty's powerful glance, as if nature left some flaw in me, some weakness, or from my side took perhaps more than enough, or upon her bestowed too much. What seems fair in all the world seems in her summed up, in her contained. Though she resembles less his image who made us both, and her form less expresses that dominion given over other creatures, yet when I approach her loveliness, so absolute she seems, so complete, so sure in herself, that what she wills to do or say seems right, wisest, best. Wisdom or reason, in dispute with her, loses."

"Do not accuse nature," said the angel. "Nature has done her part; It remains only for you to do yours. Do not lack confidence in wisdom. She will not desert you if you do not dismiss her when you need her most. Keep your self-esteem when justly grounded, and your wife will acknowledge your lead. Do not attribute too much to things less important, as you yourself perceive them to be. Her outward show is lovely, no doubt, and well worthy of your cherishing and honoring and loving, but not your subjection. And if the sense of touch whereby man procreates seems such dear delight beyond all others, remember the same faculty is given to cattle. Such would not have been given them if anything therein were worthy to subdue the soul of man or move him to passion. What in her you find worthy to love, love, for in loving you will fair well; in passion not."

Wherefore Adam pleaded, half-abashed: "But neither the loveliness of her form, nor the amorous joys of the nuptial bed delight me so much as those thousand kindnesses that daily flow from all her words and actions and declare sweet harmony in our two minds. These graces do not enslave me, but left free to choose, I choose to love, and to love you attribute me no blame, for love, you say, leads up to Heaven—is both the way and guide."

Even in mild rebuke, to speak with the angel like this was to Adam like being in Heaven, such discourse sweeter than the sweetest fruits of the palm tree. Yet unlike that fruit, it brought no satiety, but increased his hunger to hear more of the mellow voice imbued with divine grace. Adam found he could hardly still his own flow of words, perhaps meaning by example to encourage the same from his high companion.

By now they had reached the crest of that highest hill in Paradise, round which the wide Earth and sky blended in Eden's happiest view, inducing Adam to muse: "When I observe this world about me consisting of the heavens and the Earth below, and compare their magnitudes, this Earth seems but a mote against the sky and all its stars that roll across spaces incomprehensible—all to supply light for this dark Earth, this tiny spot, all their glowing energy otherwise useless. I marvel how nature could be so wasteful, to create so many grander bodies to this one use and impose on them such restless revolution repeated day by day, while the Earth—which might with far less movement pass before them instead to achieve the same end—remains motionless. She is served by worlds greater than herself, receiving her warmth and light brought by endless journey and impossible speed."

"Yet in the morning hour I set out from Heaven, where God resides, and before midday arrived in Eden," said Raphael with cheerful forbearance, "a distance inexpressible by ordinary numbers, and a journey neither wasteful nor impossible."

The comfortable summit bade them sit. The angel propped himself on rigid arms and crossed his outstretched legs. The bright pristine sky draped the horizon round. No cloud encroached. No breeze stirred the foliage, where tiny creatures lolled, unseen and silent. The pair conversed in unmitigated serenity.

"The heavens are as the book of God set before you," resumed the gracious herald, "wherein to read his wondrous works and learn his seasons, hours, days, and years. But whether it be the sky that moves or the Earth is not important. The Great Architect may not choose so soon to divulge his secrets to be scanned by those who ought rather admire. Perhaps he leaves these mysteries open to their conjecture and wide dispute hereafter to amuse himself at their various conclusions: how they will alter the mighty framework, how build, unbuild, and contrive new logic to support their cherished theories. Already your reasoning presages that of your offspring when you suppose that bodies brighter and greater should not serve the less bright. You assume that great or bright implies excellence. Yet the Earth, though small and weak in comparison, is more fruitful than the Sun, which shines barren.

"As for the heavens' wide circuit, let it speak of the Maker's high magnificence, who built an edifice so spacious, too large for man to fill, that he may know he dwells not alone, but lodged only in a small partition, the rest ordained for uses best known to his Lord. That such vast room in nature is unpossessed by living souls—deserted and desolate but for so many suns that scarcely contribute but a glimmer of light conveyed so far down to this habitat— is open to dispute. But whether these things be so, or whether not, whether the Sun rises on the Earth or the Earth on the Sun, do not trouble your thoughts. Leave hidden matters to God above. Serve him and fear him. To other creatures, wherever placed, let him attend as pleases him best. Take joy in what he gives you here: this Paradise and your mate. Heaven is too high for you to know what passes there. Be lowly wise. Think only of what concerns you and your well-being. Dream not of other worlds. Unending happiness is yours if you be found obedient and worthy of his eternal love that created you."

"How fully you satisfy my doubt," exclaimed Adam, "and guide me away from perplexing thoughts that interrupt the sweet of life, toward that prime wisdom which lies in knowing of the simple things that comprise daily life. Unchecked, the mind and fancy are apt to rove to things remote and obscure, and of their roving is no end.

"But explain why you say, 'if you be found obedient.' Can our obedience to him be found lacking, or can his love desert us whom his hands formed from dust?"

The angel leaned forward, his aspect suddenly grave.

"Son of Heaven and Earth, listen well. That you are happy is owed to God; that you continue such depends on you, on your obedience. Therein it stands. Be warned: God made you perfect, but not immutable. He made you good, but left it in your power to remain so or not. Your will is ordained free by nature, not to be overruled by fate. We of the angelic host hold our happy state as you hold yours —so long as our obedience holds and on no other certainty. He requires our voluntary service and will accept no other, for how can hearts not free show their love and their allegiance? What value lies in compulsive service, rendered in chains, or enforced by destiny? Freely we serve because freely we love. In this we stand or fall. There are those who have fallen to disobedience, and so from their high state of bliss into worst woe—from Heaven down to deepest Hell."

"Your words inspire, divine instructor," said Adam, stirred by this thrilling report, "and assure that we never shall forget to love our Maker and obey him whose single command is yet so just, though already I knew I was created free in will and deed. But your mention of some strange occurrence that has passed in Heaven moves my desire to hear more, if you consent to relate, and provided such curiosity is not impious, or notion vain, to seek illumination too high above man's vision."

The Sun had finished half his descent from apex when Raphael proceeded to grant his host's request, and in so doing, fulfill his charge to mind Adam of his condition and of his enemy. With divine narrative skill, the angel made seeable to the mind's eye of man the adventures of spirits, and revealed what might have otherwise to the human race remained hidden: how one spirit of Heaven aspired with pride and vain ambition to set himself above his peers in glory, presuming to equal in opposition the Most High; how drawing to his side many legions, he incited them to rebel with him and raise unholy war in Heaven against the throne and monarchy of

Paradise Lost

God; what violent discord befell, and how on the third day of battle, God sent Messiah, his son, with chariot and thunder to pursue Satan and all his crew to the wall of Heaven, and there hurl them headlong in horror and confusion into the great deep, down to bottomless perdition.

"Nine times the space that measures day and night to mortal men, Satan fell with his crew," Raphael concluded, "till in Hell they lay vanquished, rolling in the fiery gulf, confounded though immortal. But his doom has roused him to further wrath, for now the thought of lost happiness and lasting pain torments him. He sees and envies your state, Adam, for your race is created to fill the void left by those cast out of Heaven's kingdom, and God's favor, once his, now shines on you. Therefore, he is plotting how he may seduce you to disobedience also, that you may share his punishment and become his companion in eternal misery. This would be his solace and revenge against the Almighty. But do not listen to his temptations. Warn your wife also, who is more vulnerable, that you both profit from having heard, through terrible example, the dire reward of disobedience to those that might have stood firm, but fell. Remember, and fear to transgress."

"You have filled my ears with wonder, divine interpreter," said Adam after a pensive moment, "and revealed great things, differing far from this world, to forewarn us of what otherwise might be our loss, not knowing of events that human knowledge unaided could not reach. To the Infinite Father we owe immortal thanks for sending you to us, and receive his admonishment with solemn resolve to observe his sovereign will."

The Visitation

"I may no longer stay," pronounced the angel, rising. "The parting Sun now sets and the evening star is high, my signal to depart. Be strong, live happy, and love—most of all him whom to love is to obey. Let not passion sway your judgment. The welfare of all your sons and daughters is placed in your hands. I and all the blest of Heaven shall rejoice in your perseverance. Stand fast and repel all temptation to transgress. To stand or fall: the choice, in perfect freedom, lies within you. No outward aid do you require."

"Go if you must, heavenly messenger," said Adam. "Your teaching has been gentle and shall be ever-honored in my grateful memory. Stay friendly to mankind and visit your goodness upon him often."

And so they parted, the angel up to Heaven and Adam to his bower.

The Fall

THE SUN was sunk, and after him, Venus, the twilight star. From end to end night's hemisphere veiled the horizon round when Satan returned to Eden, bent on man's destruction. By night he had fled and at midnight returned. Three times had he circled the Earth in close pursuit of the Sun, but ever cautious of daylight, lest the watchful eye of that bright globe's vice-regent angel discover him and thwart his attempt a second time. Driven by anguish, the space of seven unbroken nights he rode with darkness, meditating fraud and malice, while searching undetected access into the garden. On the eighth, he discovered the place where the river Tigris shot into an underground gulf at the foot of Paradise, later to rise up in part as a spring by the Tree of Life. In with the river he sunk himself and up with it rose into Paradise, enveloped in rising mist, as he sought where to lie hid.

While in circling flight about the Earth, he had carefully observed every creature by moonlight to find which of all might best serve his wiles, and found the serpent, subtlest beast of all the field, fittest vessel in which to enter and hide his dark suggestions. For while cunning behavior in other beasts might betray the diabolic power within, no one would find such actions suspect in the wily snake.

So resolved, his feet embracing Earth's warm soil, he viewed the place about him, so like Heaven, if not better, worthier seat of gods, built with second thought, improving upon what was old. An earthly Heaven it was, danced round by other worlds that shined in the night, yet bore their bright lamps, light above light, for her alone it seemed. With what delight could he have walked her hills and valleys, rivers, woods and plains, if delight could find room in his poisoned heart. But he would find no place or refuge in any of these, and the more he saw of the pleasures about him, the more he felt the torment within him. All good to him becomes bane.

But neither here nor in Heaven did he seek to dwell, nor hope to lessen his misery, for only in destroying could he find ease to his relentless thoughts. So would he destroy him for whom all this was made, all of which would soon follow, linked as it was to its keeper in prosperity or woe. Man he would destroy, or win over to what would work his utter loss, that destruction wide might range. Then to the avenger alone among the infernal powers would come the glory to have marred, in one day, what cost the Almighty six in the making—six nights and days to set in motion the world that was to replace the lost throng of his adorers, which he, Satan, had in one night freed from vile servitude.

Was it that God's power to create more angels was spent, or to humiliate them the more, that he chose to bring into their vacated place a creature formed out of Earth's clay and endow him with heavenly spoils—*their* spoils? Man he made and built for him this magnificent world, pronouncing him lord of the Earth and—greatest indignity—subjecting angels to his service, to watch and minister their earthly charge. And to elude these now did Satan pry the underbrush, where he might find a sleeping serpent whose tangled folds might hide him and the dark intent he brought. Foul descent!—that he, who once contended with gods, was now constrained into a crawling beast of the slime. But what will not ambition or revenge descend to? He who aspires must bend himself as low to basest things, as high he soars. And revenge, at first sweet, before long recoils back on itself, more bitter.

"So be it," said Satan, "so long as it lands well-aimed on him who next provokes my envy, this new favorite of Heaven, this man of clay, whom his Maker raised from dust the more to spite us. Spite then with spite is best repaid."

So through each thicket, dank or dry, wrapped in creeping black vaporous mist, he held his midnight search till he found the coiled serpent sleeping, his enclosed head well-stored with subtle wiles, though not yet noxious. In through its mouth the devil entered without disturbing sleep, possessing, inspiring its brutal sense in heart and head with his own intellect, there to await the approach of morning.

†

When sacred light began to dawn in Eden, and humid flowers breathed their morning incense, the human pair came forth and filled their nostrils with sweetest smells, the season's prime, and sent up vocal praise to the Creator. This done, still Adam lingered, enamored by the charms of morning—not the least among them those especial graces sent forth by his fair consort, whose mild voice soon gently guided his thoughts to the day's work, grown large for the hands of only two, gardening so wide:

"Adam, until more hands come to our aid, the labors in this garden grow unchecked. What over-growth we prune, or prop, or bind by day, in one night or two reverts wild again with wanton growth. Perhaps more headway will be gained if we divide our labors. For, while we choose our tasks so near each other all day, looks and smiles come in between, and casual discourse interrupts and slows our work, though begun early, and the hour of supper comes quickly and unearned."

"Dear Eve," replied her mate, "nothing lovelier can be found in woman than when she strives to fulfill her domestic charge. But our Lord has not im-posed on us labor so strict as to exclude refreshment when we may need it, whether food, or talk, which is the food of the mind, or this sweet intercourse of looks and smiles, for smiles flow from reason, denied the brute, and are the food of love. He made us not only to toil, but to delight as well. Have no doubt that our joint hands will keep these paths and bowers from wilderness as wide as we need walk, till before long younger hands assist us.

"Not that brief absence is always to be shunned, for solitude is also nourishment for the soul, and short separation promises sweeter reunion. But we must not forget the warning we have received concerning that malicious foe who envies our happiness and seeks to spread his own despair. Somewhere nearby he watches, no doubt, and waits to find us separated, his best advantage to catch us unprotected from his assault, whether his first design be to draw our fidelity away from God or to disturb that which must excite his envy more than any gift enjoyed by us: our conjugal love."

Eve turned aside, as one whose love is met with some unkindness. "It saddens me to hear that you should doubt my faithfulness to God or to you," she said, her virgin majesty shaded with sweet austere composure, "simply because we have a foe who seeks to tempt it. It cannot be his violence you fear, for we are both protected from death or pain, being such as we are. His fraud is then your worry, which plainly implies that my firm faith and love can, by his fraud, be shaken or seduced. How have such sad thoughts found their way into your heart, Adam?"

"Eve, daughter of God and man," he answered, "immortal Eve—for such you are, free of all sin, all blame—it is not because I distrust your faith that I dissuade you from leaving my sight, but to avoid the attempt itself intended by our foe—for he who attempts, though in vain, insults the tempted with dishonor. You yourself would resent the offered wrong.

Paradise Lost

"Do not misjudge my wish to avert such affront to you alone. I too am in jeopardy when threatened by an enemy so subtle he could seduce angels. But he will hardly dare confront us both at once, or if he does, his assault shall fall first on me. And with you at my side, every virtue in me increases: I am more wise, more watchful, and shame at being overcome with you looking on would raise my strength, if need were of outward strength, as in strength we two unite. Why should you not feel the same when I am present, and choose to face this trial with me, best witness of your virtue tried?"

His words sought to heal, but she persisted:

"If this be our condition, to dwell in narrow limits drawn by a foe, subtle or violent, that we may not venture apart even for a moment, then perhaps he has already gained in part his hoped success. For how can we be happy if always in fear of harm? But harm comes not here to him who has not sinned.

"The low esteem of our integrity which our foe holds places no dishonor on us, but turns it back on himself and doubles our honor in Heaven's eye by proving his surmise false. For what is faith, love, or virtue untested, or tested only when sustained by exterior help? Let us not suspect our happy state has been left so imperfect and insecure by the wise Maker. Frail is our happiness if this be so, and Eden is no Eden thus exposed."

Adam took her hand in his. "Woman, you know his creating hand left nothing imperfect or deficient in all that he created, much less man or anything that might secure his happy state—secure from outward force—but within himself the danger lies. Against his will he can receive no harm, but God left free the will, for without such freedom his being must remain unfulfilled and incomplete. Yet within his freedom lies his power, and within his power lies the danger. So he bid us beware and remain alert, lest surprised by some evil appearing good, we are deceived and led to do what God expressly has forbidden. It is not mistrust then, but tender love which compels me to remind you often, and you me, that, firm in our faith as we may be, it is not impossible for us to fall into deception unawares. Why seek temptation, best avoided here with me? —for trial will come unsought, whether we be alone or together."

His argument was answered by tacit constraint, and Eve learned woman's mute power, as reluctantly he resumed with a sigh:

"But if you believe our security left untested leaves us the less secure, then go, for having you with me, not feeling free, I have you all the less. Go in your native innocence; rely on what you have of virtue; summon all, for God has done his part well; the rest is left to you."

"Do not be afraid for me, Adam." She brightened and softly withdrew her hand from his. "Nor expect a foe so proud to seek first the weaker sex, knowing failure here will shame him all the more."

Into the groves she walked, surpassing even Diana of the hunt in her goddess-like deportment, though without bow and quiver, armed instead with such gardening tools as rudimentary art had formed or angels brought. With ardent look his delighted eye pursued her long, but desired more her stay. He sent after her more than one plea for her quick return, and she promised to have noon meal prepared and waiting for him in the bower, leaving afternoon's sweet repose theirs to share.

Alas, never from that hour in Paradise was found either sweet repast or sound repose! Ambush hid among the flowers to intercept her way and send her back despoiled of innocence. For now, and since first break of dawn, had the fiend, mere serpent in appearance, pursued his quest in field and grove, by fountain or by shady stream, wherever some pleasant garden plot might invite the master and mistress of the land to pass their hours. He sought them both, but wished luck might find them separate, though little hoped, when to his wish, beyond hope, he spied her alone, veiled in a cloud of fragrance where she stood, so thick the roses glowed around her. Each gay flower of slender drooping stalk she gently uplifted and tied with a band of myrtle. Carnation, purple, azure, and gold they were —herself the fairest unsupported flower, so far from her own best support and mindless of the storm so near.

Nearer he drew, now boldly crossing walks sheltered by stately cedar and pine, now disappearing among the thick woven shrubs and flowers bordering each path, the handiwork of Eve. Such pleasure took the serpent to behold her heavenly form among the flowery plot—angelic, but more soft in graceful innocence—that her every gesture or least action subdued his malice and robbed his fierceness of the fierce intent it brought. Thus transported in that space, the evil one stood abstracted from his own evil, and for a time remained entranced, disarmed of enmity, of guile, hate, envy, or revenge. But the hot hell that always in him burns, even in mid-

Heaven, soon ended his delight and brought back his torture, the more he saw of pleasure not intended for his taste. Fierce hate regrew and returned all thoughts of mischief, to destroy all pleasure save that which is had in destroying. Alone, the woman, vulnerable to all attempts, now offered him opportunity that must not pass, for nowhere in view was her more formidable partner, endowed with strength and proud courage, built of heroic limb and exempt from wound—not unlike Satan once was in Heaven, though now enfeebled by Hell's pain.

Across the ground, towards Eve, he wound his way with indented waves, not prone as his kind now moves, debased by his act, but rising in circular folds that towered fold above fold in a surging maze, his head crested high aloft, with jeweled eyes on burnished neck of green and gold, erect amidst his circling spirals. Never since has serpent kind more dazzling slid the earth. With oblique approach at first, as one who seeks access but hesitates to interrupt, sidelong he worked his varied way and curled many a wanton wreath in his tortuous train in sight of Eve, to lure her eye. Preoccupied, she heard the sound of rustling leaves but took no mind, as she was used to the playful movements of animals in the garden. Bolder now, he stood before her, bowing his sleek enameled neck as if in admiring gaze, fawning, and licking the ground on which she trod. His gentle expression at length turned the eye of Eve. Her attention gained, his serpent tongue turned organ of voice, and his fraudulent temptation thus began:

"Do not be startled, mistress, that I approach you unsummoned and gaze enchanted, unable to look away. All living things adore your celestial beauty, universally admired, masterwork of our Great Maker. But here in this wild enclosure, among these beasts too crude to witness half your beauty, who sees you but one man, and what is one to her who should be seen, adored, and served by numberless angels—a goddess among gods."

"What can this mean?" she exclaimed, amazed at the voice and not unswayed by the smooth flattery. "Language of man pronounced by tongue of brute, and human sense expressed! I thought all beasts were created mute to all articulate sound and denied the ability to reason (though in their looks and action often appears much sense). I know the serpent to be subtlest of all beasts, but not endowed with human voice. How did this miracle come about?"

"Empress of this fair world," replied the guileful reptile, "I was at first like the other beasts that graze the trodden herb: of low thoughts, concerned little beyond food or sex, and apprehending nothing high —till on a day roving the field, I chanced upon a tree laden with fruit of fairest red and gold. I drew nearer to gaze, when from the boughs a savory smell blew over me. Hunger and thirst quickened in me at the scent of those alluring apples. About the mossy trunk I wound, for those high branches would require your utmost reach, or Adam's. Round the tree all the other beasts that saw but could not reach stood longing and envying. Until that hour, never had I found such pleasure at feed or fountain. I ate my fill, and before long perceived strange alterations within myself. Though outwardly I remained the same, powers of reason and speech grew within. To speculations high and deep I turned my thoughts, to all matters concerning Heaven or Earth, and considered all things visible on Earth, all fair, all good. With your approach, all things fair and good withered before your divine beauty that has no equivalent or second, supreme of creatures, mistress of the universe."

Yet more amazed, the unwary Eve responded:

"Serpent, your overpraising leaves in doubt the quality of sense imparted by that fruit. But tell me, where grows this tree, how far from here? Many of the varied trees of Paradise are yet unknown to us, in such abundance lies our choice."

"Empress, the way is not long: beyond a row of myrtles, on a flat near a fountain, past one small thicket of blossoming myrrh and balsam; I can soon lead you there."

And forthwith, on he swiftly rolled in waves and made the intricate way seem straight, anxious to swift mischief, his brightened crest elevated in hope, anticipating joy. She followed, led by fraud, to the tree that was to become the root of all sorrow. Learning their destination, her interest ebbed:

"Serpent, we might have spared our coming here. I know this tree, for God has commanded that of its fruit we may not taste nor touch—his sole commandment."

"Indeed?" the tempter replied. "Has God not said you should eat of the fruit of every garden tree, declared lords of all the Earth?"

To which, Eve returned these words, the last from lips yet sinless:

"We may eat of the fruit of every tree in the garden, but of this fair tree that grows in its center, God has said we should not eat, nor should we touch it, or we will die."

Paradise Lost

The tempter, more bold with show of zeal and love to man and indignation at his wrong, now played a new role. He moved his uncoiled form in eloquent undulations, as if raised by passion, like some great orator in Athens or Rome about to begin on some great matter.

"Oh sacred, wise, and wisdom-giving plant, mother of knowledge, now I feel your power clear within me, not only to discern things in their causes, but to trace the motives of Heaven's highest agents, deemed however wise! Queen of the universe, do not believe those rigid threats of death. You shall not die. How could you? By the fruit? Through knowledge, it gives you life. By the threatener? Look at me, who have touched and tasted, yet not only live, but, by venturing higher than my lot, have attained life more perfect than ever fate meant for me. Shall God be angered by such a petty trespass, or rather praise your dauntless virtue which denounces threat of death in pursuit of higher knowledge—knowledge of good and evil? What evil can be in knowing good? For good unknown surely is not to be had, or had and yet unknown, is not really had at all. And of evil—if what is evil be real, why not know it, since a known enemy is more easily avoided?

"Why then is this fruit forbidden? Why, but to keep you low and ignorant: his worshipers. He knows that in the day you eat thereof, your eyes shall be opened and you shall be as gods, knowing good and evil as they know. As I have become like man, so in like proportion you shall become like a god. It is true you may die the death of humanity, but only to be reborn a god—a death to be wished. What are gods that man may not become as they?

The Fall

They came first, and by that advantage would have us believe that all proceeds from them. I question it, for I see this fair Earth, warmed by the Sun, producing every kind; them, nothing. If they create all things, then who was it that enclosed knowledge in this tree, that whosoever eats thereof forthwith attains wisdom without their aid? And wherein lies the offense that man should aspire to knowledge? What can your knowledge hurt him above, or this tree impart against his will, if all be in his power? Or does envy dwell in heavenly breasts? These questions and more argue your need of this fair answering fruit. Reach then, earthly goddess, and freely taste."

Into her heart too easy entrance won his words, replete with guile. She gazed fixedly at the fruit, which to behold might tempt alone, as in her ears yet rang the sound of his persuasive voice, imbued with reason and truth, or so it seemed. Meanwhile the hour of noon drew on and wakened eager appetite, raised by the smell so savory of that fruit where fell her longing eye.

She looked and admired its virtues, doubtless best of fruits, with taste too long kept from man, taste that taught the tongue not made for speech to speak its praise. Even he who forbad its use did not deny its virtue, arousing desire all the more by his forbidding, which implied some secret good inherent. Wisdom forbidden? Such prohibitions could not be binding. In the day she would eat of that fair fruit, her pronounced doom was she would die, yet the serpent had eaten and lived, and knew, and spoke, and reasoned, and discerned, and envied not, but brought with joy the good befallen him, friendly to man. What had she then to fear, or rather, what could she know to fear under this ignorance of good and evil, of God or death, of law and penalty? Here grew the cure of all, fruit divine, fair to the eye, inviting to the taste, with powers to make wise. What prevented her then to reach and feed at once both body and mind?

So reasoning, in this evil hour, her rash hand forth reaching to the fruit, she plucked.

She ate.

Earth felt the wound, and Nature, from her seat, sighing through all her works, gave signs of woe that all was lost.

Back to the thicket slunk the guilty serpent unnoticed, for Eve was intent now wholly on her taste, such delight till now it seemed she had never tasted, whether true or imagined so through high expectation. She swallowed greedily, without restraint, not knowing she ate death. Satiated at length and heightened as with wine, to herself she expressed great satisfaction in her deed:

"Oh most precious of all trees in Paradise, worthy of highest praise, henceforth often shall I ease the burden of your branches, till on your diet I grow mature in knowledge, as a god who knows all things, though others envy what they cannot give, for had the gift been theirs to give, it would not grow here with fair fruit left to hang as if to no end created."

But to Adam how would she appear, she wondered. Should she make known to him her change and give him to partake full happiness with her? Or rather not, but keep the odds of knowledge in her favor that rendered her superior? Would her higher state draw his worship and love all the greater, or would his inferiority make him resentful and envious, that ultimately he would come to hate her? Could goddesses find discourse with men, or share their beds?

Heaven was high and remote to see distinctly each thing on Earth, and other cares perhaps might divert the Great Forbidder and all his spies from continual watch, but if God had seen, and death ensued, then she would be no more, and Adam wedded to another Eve. His joy thus resumed after her death was as unthinkable to her as was his hate towards her in life. "Resolved then, I confirm," said she: "Adam shall share with me, whether in bliss or woe. So dear I love him that with him all deaths I could endure; without him, live no life."

✝

Adam, the while awaiting her return, had woven a garland of choicest florets to adorn her tresses and crown her garden labors, as reapers do their harvest queen. Great joy he promised to his thoughts in her return so long delayed. Yet his heart faltered, and misgivings of something ill sent him forth to find her. Following the way she took that morning when first they parted, his search must bring him by the Tree of Knowledge, and there he found her, in her hand a bough of fairest downy fruit, newly picked, diffusing ambrosial smell.

"Adam, have you wondered at my stay?" she greeted him, her voice too cheery and face flushed like a child surprised in her mischief. "I have missed your presence and learned the agony of love till now not felt: the pain of absence from your sight. But strange has been the cause of my delay, and wonderful to hear. Adam, this tree is not as we are told, not a tree of danger, nor opening the way to unknown evil, but of divine effect, to open eyes and make them gods who taste."

As she spoke, from his slack hand the garland wreath dropped and all the faded roses scattered. Paralyzed and blank he stood. Horror chill ran through his veins, till at length he found speech to silence hers and forestall fate:

"You have not tasted! Some cursed, fraudulent enemy has beguiled you! Say you have not violated the sacred fruit forbidden, and remains undone what once past none can recall or done undo!"

"No enemy, Adam, but the friendly serpent," came her pacific reply, "made wise by taste of the fruit—not dead, as we were threatened, but endowed with human voice and human sense, worthy of admiration. So persuasively did he reason with me, that I also tasted and have found similar mind-expanding effect. My eyes are more open, my heart more full, my spirits dilated."

Speechless he stood, and pale, till passion again broke forth to animate his grief:

"Oh fairest of creation, last and best of all God's works, how are you lost? How suddenly lost? Defaced, deflowered, and doomed to death!

"But perhaps you will not die. Perhaps the deed is not so heinous now, the fruit having been foretasted by the serpent and profaned by him, made common and unhallowed. I cannot think that God will in earnest destroy us, his prime creatures, set above all his works, all for us created, all of which, in our death, must also die. If God can and must uncreate and undo, better he should undo the transgression, or uncreate the serpent, never to have tempted, or abolish the tree, sacred or cursed."

But she remained placid, despite the guilty glow in her cheek, and smiled, as might a mother to her frightened child.

"Do you see in me a corpse, Adam, for such grief your words and face express? Yet I feel twice alive and awake as before. Or can it be that already I transcend to levels above man's low perception. Such levels have I aspired to and sought mainly for you, for without you all is truly lost. All shared with you is bliss, which unshared, soon becomes tedious and hateful. You must eat also, that equal lot may join us in equal joy, as equal love. If not, we shall be separated by mismatched degree. Then I, too late, will renounce my deed done for you and take up your vain cry to undo."

Wherefore did Adam submit to that which seemed without remedy:

"I have fixed my lot with you, my wife, certain to undergo the same doom. If death comes to you, dear Eve, then death is to me as life, and life is living death. For how can I live without you? How can I forgo your sweet companionship and love so dearly joined, left behind in these empty woods? Should God create another Eve and I afford another rib, yet never will the loss of you from my heart be relieved, so forcibly I feel the bond of nature that draws me to my own in you. Our state cannot be severed, for what you are is mine, bone of my bone, flesh of my flesh; we are one. To lose you is to lose myself. Therefore, my resolution is certain: with you, to die."

Paradise Lost

She embraced him, deeply moved by this example of his exceeding love. "Oh Adam, this glorious day affords good proof of our glad union whereof you speak—one heart, one soul in both, linked in love so dear, as evidenced by your declared resolve to undergo with me one guilt, one crime, if any be in tasting this fair fruit, from which still further good comes: this happy trial of your love, which otherwise might never be thus shown. Oh faithful love unequaled!

"Yet if I thought death would ensue from this attempt, I would alone sustain the worst and not persuade you join me. Rather would I die alone than pull you into jeopardy with me or render you liable for my deed. But I see far different outcome: not death, but life heightened for us both, eyes opened to new hopes, new joys so divine that what sweet taste has touched our sense before will seem flat and harsh to this. Trust from my experience, Adam, freely taste, and cast all fear of death to the winds."

From the bough she gave him of the fair enticing fruit, his dubious reward. Against his better knowledge, overcome with female charm, he did not hesitate to eat. Earth trembled from her entrails again in pangs, and Nature gave a second groan. The sky frowned, and muttering thunder, wept some sad drops at the completing of the mortal sin original, while Adam took no thought, eating his fill, joined by Eve, who, desiring to soothe and encourage him, did not fear to repeat her trespass.

Now intoxicated as with new wine, both swam in mirth and fancied they felt divinity within them, breeding angel wings with which to soar the Earth. But that false fruit brought forth far different effect, as new appetite quickened in each, inflaming carnal desire. Adam cast lascivious eyes on Eve, and she as wantonly repaid him. In lust they burned, till he began to toy with her:

"Eve, now I see how exacting is your taste, how elegant. In providing this day's meal you have out-done yourself. I yield to you all praise. Much pleasure have we lost abstaining from this delightful fruit so rich in seasoned wisdom, nor have we known till now true relish in tasting, as we savor each delicious meaning. If such pleasure be in things forbidden, it might be wished, instead of this one tree, had been forbidden ten.

"Now come to me, fair bounty of this generous tree, fairer now than ever, and let us play after such fine fare; for never, since the day first I beheld you, adorned with all perfection, has your beauty so in-flamed my senses with warm passion to enjoy."

He seized her hand with look of sexual intent, well-understood by Eve, whose eye darted conta-gious fire, and led her to a shady bank, thick over-head with green enclosure. Flowers were the couch, pansies and violets, lilies and hyacinth, Earth's fresh-est, softest lap. There, without restraint, they took their fill of love's diversion, the consummation of their mutual guilt, till, exhausted by their amorous play, deep sleep oppressed them both.

Soon the smooth exhilarating vapor of that de-ceptive fruit was all exhaled, and grosser dreams overtook and burdened their unnatural sleep. They woke as from unrest, and each viewing the other soon found in what unexpected way their eyes had been opened. Innocence, which like a veil had shad-owed them from knowing ill, was gone, and with it all confidence and natural grace, leaving them naked to guilty shame. Destitute and bare of all their virtue, they sat long and silent, confounded, as if stricken mute, till Adam, though no less ashamed than his consort, at length gave these strained words utterance:

"Our eyes are opened, Eve, and indeed we know both good and evil—good lost and evil got, bad fruit of knowledge, if this be knowledge which leaves us naked like this, void of honor, of innocence, grace, purity.

"How shall I behold the face of God or angel, so often beheld with joy and rapture? Those heavenly shapes will blind now with their blaze insufferably bright. But that I might live here in solitude, in some obscure glade where highest wood impenetrable to Sun or starlight might hide me, that I might never see them more!

"Let us quickly devise some way to hide this new found bodily shame, offensive to Heaven and to each other—some tree whose broad leaves sewn together and banded round our loins will cover these middle parts that suddenly reproach us as unclean."

Both together went into the thickest wood and there chose the fig tree of that kind whose broad leaves like Amazon shields spread coolest shade. Those they gathered in vain attempt to cover their guilt and dreadful shame. This done, but not at rest or ease of mind, they sat and wept. Nor only did tears rain at their eyes, but worse winds began to rise within: high passions, anger, hate, mistrust, and suspicion. Discord shook sore their inward state of mind, regions once calm and full of peace, now tossed and turbulent. Estranged in look, Adam first unleashed his distemper:

"If only had you heeded me and stayed with me this morning as I urged when that strange desire of wandering possessed you from I know not where, then might we remain still happy. Oh, let men not seek needless cause to prove their faith! So we have dearly learned: when earnestly they seek such proof, then do they begin to fail."

"What severe words pass your lips, Adam," returned Eve, "ascribing to my fault, or will of wandering as you call it, what who knows but might have happened as easily with you beside me. You could have discerned fraud in the serpent no more than I, speaking as he did.

"Was I never to have parted from your side, as good as grown there, still a lifeless rib? If I were so unworthy of your trust, why did you not command me absolutely not to go, headed into such danger as you said? Then, too easily swayed, you did not much oppose me. Had you been firm, I would not have transgressed, nor you with me."

Enraged, Adam assailed her: "Is this the love repaid to mine, ungrateful woman, which I expressed when you were lost, not I, who might have lived and enjoyed immortal bliss, yet willingly chose rather to die with you? Now I am reproached as the cause of your transgression, that I was not firm enough in restraining you. What more could I have done? I warned you. I foretold the danger and the lurking enemy to be feared. Beyond this could only be the use of force to keep you, and force upon free will has no place here. But confidence bore you boldly on, whether expecting to meet no danger or hoping to find opportunity for glorious trial in confrontation. And perhaps I was also wrong in overly admiring what seemed in you so perfect that I thought no evil could touch you. I regret that error now which has become my crime, and you my accuser.

"Let this be a lesson to him that allows the will of a woman to rule. She will not endure restraint, but left to herself and finding evil the result, will turn and accuse his weak indulgence."

And so they spent the fruitless hours in mutual accusation, and of their vain contest appeared no end.

XI

Judgment

UP INTO HEAVEN the angelic guards ascended, silent and sad for man, for they perceived his fallen state. At Heaven-gate, where the multitudes had gathered to hear how all befell, the faces of the blessed populace, accustomed to unviolated bliss, were not spared dim sadness now—yet mixed with pity and much wondering how the subtle fiend had stolen entrance into Paradise unseen. Toward the Supreme Throne the accountable made haste to plea their guiltlessness and attest their unbroken vigilance. Their plea was easily approved even before they spoke, for their judge was omniscient, all-seeing, all-knowing. Amidst thunderous rumblings from his secret cloud, the voice of the Eternal Father issued forth:

"Assembled angels, and powers returned from unsuccessful charge, be not troubled or dismayed by these tidings of mishap from Earth which your sincerest care could not prevent. Man was left to his free will, its inclination untouched with lightest moment of impulse by me. But fallen he is, and now it remains that mortal sentence pass on his transgression.

"To judge them I send you, Vicegerent Son, to whom I have transferred all judgment, whether in Heaven, Earth, or Hell. Easily it can be seen that I intend to let justice unite with mercy in sending you, man's friend, his mediator and volunteered Redeemer, destined to be himself man, now to judge man fallen."

In unfolding glory blazing bright on his right hand, the benign Son answered:

"Eternal Father, for you it is to decree; for me to do your will, both in Heaven and Earth. I shall go to judge these sinners, tempering with mercy high justice, as may fulfill both in their proper light, yet knowing the worst of this judgment must fall back on me when the time shall come. So I vowed before you and stand committed without regret, that I may divert their doom, that you may ever rest well-pleased. No attendants or train is needed, for none need behold the judgment but the two judged. The third is best absent, already convicted by his flight, condemned rebel to all law."

From his radiant seat of high collateral glory, he rose and was accompanied as far as Heaven-gate by the thrones and powers, princedoms and dominations, his ministers. From there, Eden and all the coast lay in view. Straight down he descended with speed not counted by time. The Sun was falling low in the west, and gentle afternoon breezes fanned the Earth, when the mild Judge and Intercessor came to sentence man. As evening's cool approached, the soft winds of declining day brought to human ears the voice of God in the garden, and they hid themselves from his presence, both man and wife, among the thickest trees. As God approached, he called aloud, "Where are you, Adam? Why do you not come forth with your accustomed greeting, always so joyfully expressed at my coming seen far off ?"

Forth he came, and with him Eve, more hesitant now though first to sin. Both were of wretched countenance. Love was not in their looks, either to God or to each other, but guilt and shame and despair and anger and hate and guile. Through heavy silence, Adam broke falteringly:

"I heard you in the Garden and was afraid of your voice, and being naked, hid myself."

"Often have you heard my voice," said God, "and not been afraid, but rejoiced to hear it. How has it become so dreadful to you? And who told you that you are naked? Have you eaten of the tree whereof I have forbidden you should eat?"

To which, painfully Adam replied, "Oh Heaven! This day I stand before my Judge, accountable, either to undergo myself the insupportable weight of total blame, or to accuse my other self, the partner of my life, whose failing, as her protector, I should conceal. This woman that you made to be my help and gave me as your perfect gift, so good, so fit, so divine that from her hand I could suspect no ill—and whatever she did, in itself her doing seemed to justify the deed—she gave me the fruit of the tree, and I did eat."

Paradise Lost

"Was she your god?" said he, sole God and Judge, "that you obeyed her voice before his, or had she become superior to you, that you relinquished your manhood to her, resigning the place wherein God set you above her made from you. She was endowed with loveliness indeed, but to attract your love, not your subjection. Her gifts were in nature to be supportive, but unseemly to bear rule, which was your part had you truly known yourself." And turning to Eve, he asked, "Woman, what is it you have done?"

Overwhelmed with shame, Eve confessed: "The serpent beguiled me, and I did eat."

The Lord God, hearing this, without delay proceeded to judgment on the accused serpent, though mere instrument of him who devised the mischief, accursed nevertheless and debased in nature:

"Because you have done this, you are condemned beneath all cattle and each beast of the field. Upon your belly groveling shall you go, and dust shall you eat all the days of your life. Between you and the woman I will cast enmity, and between yours and her seed. Her seed shall bruise your head, as you shall bruise his heel."

He then turned his sentence upon the woman:

"Greatly will I multiply your sorrow by your conception. In sorrow shall you bring forth children, and to your husband's will shall you submit, for he shall rule over you."

Last, on Adam he pronounced judgment:

"Because you have heeded the voice of your wife and have eaten of the tree whereof I commanded you should not eat, cursed is the ground from which it grew, and in sorrow shall you eat thereof all the days of your life. Thorns also and thistles shall it bring forth to you unwelcomed. In the sweat of your face shall you eat bread until you return to the ground, for out of it were you taken. From dust you come and to dust shall you return."

So did he judge man, sent as both Judge and Savior. But mercifully holding back the instant stroke of death now due, he removed it far off from that day. And pitying how they stood before him, naked to the air, aware and ashamed, he did not hesitate to assume the place of servant. As father of his family, he clothed their nakedness with skins of beasts slain; nor did he neglect their inward nakedness, much more shameful, but covered it from his Father's sight with his robe of righteousness. Then with swift ascent he returned to him in Heaven, who, though all-knowing and appeased, heard recounted to him what had passed with man and woman, with sweet intercession added in their behalf.

†

While sin was thus committed and judged on Earth, down below the gates at the mouth of Hell stood wide open, belching outrageous flames far into Chaos, unmoved since passed through by the fiend. On opposite sides the sentinel pair sat, till Sin, opening, to Death began:

"Son, why do we sit here idly watching each other, while Satan, our great author, thrives in other worlds, seeking a happier seat for us? It cannot be that anything but success accompanies him. If not, he would be returned before this, driven with fury by his avengers, since no place but this can fit his punishment or their revenge. Moreover, I feel a new strength rise within me, wings growing, and large dominion opening to me beyond this deep. Whatever draws me on—intuitive sense of victory, or some powerful force that transcends distance to unite in sympathetic understanding things of like kind—you, my inseparable shade, must come with me.

"It may be the difficulty of passing back over this impenetrable gulf that delays his return. Let us try to establish a pathway over this deep, from Hell to that new world where Satan now prevails. Such work would be a monument of high merit to all the infernal host, easing their future passage forth and back. I cannot fail to find the way, so strongly am I drawn by this new felt attraction."

With nostrils upturned to the murky air, the meager shadow answered, delighting in the smell of mortal change on Earth:

"Go where fate and your inclination lead; I will not lag far behind, such a scent I draw of carnage and prey innumerable, and taste the savor of death from all things there that live. To the work you propose, though disagreeable to my nature and yours, I will afford you equal aid."

Then both flew out from Hell's gates into the wide wasteful anarchy of Chaos, like ravenous fowl lured with scent of living carcasses designed for death. Hovering upon the raging sea, from each side they drove all tossed substance solid or slimy towards the brink of Hell. With his staff, Death beat the aggregate soil, fixing the slime into cold, dry asphalt. The gathered beach they fastened firm to the roots of Hell, and upon this foundation formed the immense arch over the foaming deep, a bridge of prodigious length joined to the immovable wall of this now defenseless universe, forfeit to Death, leaving open a broad, smooth, easy passage down to Hell. A wondrous ridge of suspended rock it was, following the track of Satan to the selfsame place where he first safe lighted out of Chaos onto this bare cosmic shell. Here they made fast the arch, permanently anchored with deep stakes. Henceforth, three ways met here in crossroads, Heaven's natural link with this world now interposed on the left hand with Hell's long reach.

From here the pair were about to make their way down toward Paradise, when they beheld the likeness of a bright angel steering his way between the constellations of Centaur and the Scorpion, discretely distant from the rising Sun in Aries. Despite his disguise, those children soon discerned their parent. After seducing Eve, Satan had slunk unnoticed into the nearby wood, and changing shape, watched his guileful act seconded by her upon her husband. He had witnessed their shame that sought vain excuses, but when the Son of God descended to judge them, had fled, terrified, not hoping to escape, but to shun for the present what God's sudden wrath might inflict. Returning by night, he had listened where the hapless pair sat, and from their sad discourse, gathered that his own doom was not to be here felt, but long delayed. Now, joyfully returning to Hell, near the foot of this new wondrous structure at the brink of Chaos, he saw his offspring cheerfully come to meet him. At the sight of that stupendous bridge, Satan's joy increased, and he stood long admiring, till his fair enchanting daughter broke the silence:

"Father, view the trophy of your own magnificent deeds. Of this great bridge, you are the prime architect. When in my heart, which by secret harmony still moves with yours, I felt that you had prospered on Earth, as your looks now confirm, I was compelled to come after you with your son. Hell could no longer hold us in her bounds, so irresistibly were we drawn, nor this obscure, impassable gulf deter our way, so great had grown our strength. With ease did we overlay the dark abyss with this highway, following your illustrious track. You have achieved our liberty and empowered us to do your work. Your virtue has won what our hands have built. All this world is now yours. You have fully avenged our defeat in Heaven. Your wisdom has gained what war has lost. Here you shall reign monarch. There let him rule, adjudged victor in battle, but from this new world let him retire, alienated by his own condemnation. Henceforth, he will divide monarchy with you between two worlds, and find you more dangerous to his throne, though far removed."

To this, the glad prince of darkness answered:

"Fair daughter, and you, both son and grandchild, together you have given high proof of the ample merit in the race of Satan and all the infernal empire, as so near Heaven's door you meet my triumphal act with one of your own, this glorious work. You have joined into one realm Hell and this world, made exposed and vulnerable by my exploit, henceforth one continent of easy thoroughfare. Now, while I return with ease on your road through darkness to my associate powers, you two descend among these numerous planets, all yours, right down to Paradise. Live there and reign in bliss, and exercise dominion on Earth and in the air, but chiefly on man, falsely declared sole lord of all. Him shall you first enslave, and lastly kill. I will send my deputies and create a force on Earth of matchless might issuing from me. My hold of this new kingdom depends on your joined effort. If your dual power prevails, the affairs of Hell need fear no loss. Go, and be strong."

He dismissed them, and with speed they held their course, spreading their poison through thickest constellations. The damned stars paled, and the planets then suffered deadly eclipse. Satan went the other way down the causeway to Hell-gate, as on either side, Chaos, dispossessed, assailed the unyielding structure with rebounding waves of indignation. Through the gate, wide open and unguarded, Satan passed and found all about him desolate, for those appointed to sit there had left their charge. The rest were all retired far to the inland, about the walls of Pandemonium, city and proud seat of Lucifer fallen, having done such wandering in their dismal world as, in his absence, inclination or sad choice had led them, seeking peace to restless thoughts and to entertain the irksome hours.

In squadrons and thick bands had they set forth in his path to discover Hell's limits and if perhaps some new region might yield them easier habitation. Four ways they had bent their flying march, along the banks of four infernal rivers that disgorge their baleful streams into the burning lake that is Hell's middle: Abhorred Styx, the flood of deadly hate; sad Acheron, of sorrow black and deep; Cocytus, named for loud lamentation heard on its rueful stream; and fierce Phlegethon, whose waves of torrent fire inflame with rage. Far off from these, a slow and silent stream, Lethe, the river of oblivion, rolls her watery labyrinth. He who drinks thereof forthwith forgets his former state and being, forgets both joy and grief, pleasure and pain. Beyond this, a frozen continent lies, dark and wild, beat with perpetual storms of whirlwind and dire hail, which falls on firm land and thaws not, but gathers in heaps that resemble ancient ruins. All is deep snow and ice here, a profound gulf that could sink whole armies. The parching air burns frigid, and cold performs the effect of fire, more bitterly felt by change of fierce extremes. Perplexed, the powers had here disbanded, wandering to seek some place of healing warmth or cool recess, but finding none. Those who passed the tempting stream would struggle to reach, with one small drop to lose in sweet forgetfulness all pain and woe, all in a moment, and so near the brink, but fate would not allow, for here, of its own accord, the water retreats and dries at approach of living thirst, or sudden hideous creatures emerge to guard the bank with undiscovered terrors. Thus roving on in confused march had the adventurous bands with shuddering horror first viewed their lamentable lot, and found no rest. Through many a dark and dreary valley they marched, over many a frozen, many a fiery alp. Rocks, caves, lakes, bogs, dens, and shades of death—a universe of death, which God by curse created evil. For evil, only such is good. Where all life dies, death lives, and nature breeds perverse, all monstrous, all prodigious things, abominable, un-utterable, and worse than fables yet have shaped or fear conceived: gorgons, and hydras, and chimeras dire.

Little wonder now to find the whole congregation here self-confined on castle grounds, all wanderlust quenched, their excess vigor transferred to bold debate. There the legions had kept their careful watch round the metropolis, while the grand council sat expecting each hour their great emperor's return, apprehensive what chance might intercept his adventure. Now through the council midst in that plutonian hall he passed unseen, in guise matching the lowest order of military angel. At the upper end, under regal spread of richest display, he ascended his high throne and sat awhile unperceived, and watched in silence.

Much arguing among his restless bands filled the unquiet hall. The discord was amicable, the topics questions of good and evil, of happiness and final misery, passion and apathy, and glory and shame, with much high reasoning on providence, foreknowledge, will, and fate—fixed fate, free will, foreknowledge absolute—vain wisdom all, and false philosophy, all logic lost in wandering mazes, yet such pleasing meandering as would stay anguish, conjure false hope, and arm the hardened breast with stubborn patience against the anxious wait on the all important mission of their king. At last his radiant head and star-bright shape emerged as from a dispersing cloud, clad with what false glitter was left him since his fall. So sudden was the blaze that the startled throng drew back in shock. In amazement, all beheld their mighty chief returned. The consulting peers rushed forth with loud acclaim, till his raised hand and these words silenced them:

"Thrones, dominations, princedoms, virtues, powers—I call you by your titles repossessed, for I return successful beyond hope, to lead you forth, triumphant, out of this infernal pit, to possess as lords a spacious world little inferior to our native

Paradise Lost

Heaven. I could relate at length my hard adventure that achieved this, and with what long struggles I voyaged the vast unbounded deep, whose horrible confusion you are spared, for now it lies traversed by a broad way paved by Sin and Death, my heirs, to expedite your glorious march. I was forced to ride the fathomless abyss unguided, where night without origin and wild Chaos fiercely opposed my journey, jealous of their secrets. I found the new created world whose creation had in Heaven long been foretold, a fabric wonderful, of absolute perfection. Therein resided man, happily secluded in a Paradise of pleasure, his place won by our exile. By fraud, I seduced him from his Creator—this done, laughably, with an apple. Alas, by this he above was sorely offended and has given up both his beloved man and all his world, now prey to Sin and Death, and so to us, to range and to dwell and rule over man and over all he should have ruled. Me also did he judge, or rather, not me, but the brute serpent in whose shape I deceived man. My punishment is man's hatred. I am to bruise his heel. His seed— when is not known—shall bruise my head. A world is ours at the purchase price of a bruise! Such was my quest. What remains but for you to rise and reap its rewards?"

He stood, expecting their universal shout and high applause, but instead a dismal hiss filled his ear, the sound of public scorn. Before he could wonder at this, a stranger phenomenon distracted him. He felt his body contract and tighten, his arms cling to his ribs, his legs entwine each other, till toppling, down he fell, a monstrous serpent on his belly, struggling but in vain. A greater power ruled him now, punishing him in the shape in which he had sinned. He would speak, but his effort produced a hiss, joining the universal din, for now all were alike transformed into serpents, all accessories to his crime. Dreadful was the hissing through the hall, thickly swarming with intertwining bodies, varied in their hideousness: scorpions and asps; vipers horned and fanged; pythons, headed at each end; and Satan in the midst, a dragon, still king on the slithering, living carpet. Out to the open field they all followed him, where the remainder of his legions stood in sharp array, with eager anticipation to see their glorious chief issuing forth in triumph. Instead they saw emerge a swarm of ugly serpents. Their horror quickly grew, for what they saw, they felt themselves become. Down fell both shield and spear, and they as fast. The dire hiss renewed, and the transfiguration spread like a flood.

To aggravate their penance, a tree sprang up nearby laden with fair fruit like that which grew in Paradise, the bait of Eve. As their eyes fixed intent on that strange prospect, there rose about them a whole forest of forbidden trees to work them further woe and shame. Now parched with scalding thirst and fierce hunger, on they rolled into the grove in heaps and up the trees, which were soon thickly hung like the snaky locks of Medusa. Greedily biting, they attacked the fruit with relish, eager to allay their appetite, but instead chewed bitter ashes, which the offended taste rejected with spattering sounds. Then, falling into the same illusion, hunger and thirst and the irresistible sight and scent, again in spasms they writhed, their jaws filled with soot and cinders. Often they lapsed, not as man, who fell once, but with repeated deceits, temptations, and dismay. Thus were they long plagued till, worn with famine, they were permitted to resume their lost shape, cursed, some say, to undergo this humbling torment each year for certain numbered days, to dash their pride and joy over man's seduction. Others hold that they soon dispersed among the heathen descendants of their first earthly victims, intermingling, and spreading wide their venom.

✝

Meanwhile, the hellish pair arrived in Paradise —Sin already there in action, now in body, seeking permanent dwelling; behind her, Death close following pace for pace, not mounted yet on his pale horse.

"What do you think now of our empire?" she asked her all-conquering offspring. "Is it not much better here than to sit watch at Hell's dark threshold, unnamed, unfeared, and yourself half-starved?"

The sin-bred monster answered: "To me, whose hunger is eternal and insatiable, Hell, Paradise, or Heaven all are alike. Wherever I may meet the more abundant prey is best, which here, though soon to become plentiful, now seems all too little to stuff this stomach or fill this bone-starved corpse with flesh."

"Feed then on these herbs and fruits and flowers first," was her maternal advice; "next on each beast and fish and fowl. Spare no morsel made weak and ripe by time, till I, residing in man throughout his race, infect all his thoughts, his looks, words, and actions, and season him, your last and sweetest prey."

Then they both wandered their separate ways, to destroy, or for certain destruction, mortalize all that had been immortal.

"See with what heat these dogs of Hell advance," the Almighty, watching from his transcendent seat among the saints, declared to his concordant son, and for all to hear. "Smugly they approach their quarry, scented from so far, to waste and bring havoc to that world which I created so fair and good, and would have forever kept in that state had not the folly of man let in these wasteful furies. That folly they ascribe to me, as do the prince of Hell and his adherents, as if in some fit of passion I had yielded all to their misrule, permitting them to enter with so much ease and possess the world, ignorant that I called and drew them there, my scavenging hell-hounds, to lick up the draff and filth which man's polluting sin has shed on what was pure, till crammed and gorged near bursting with sucked and swallowed refuse, unexpectedly they find themselves hurled back through Chaos by one sling of your victorious arm to the mouth of Hell, obstructing and forever sealing up with their glutted bodies its ravenous jaws. Then shall Heaven and renewed Earth be made pure to sanctity that shall receive no further stain."

The heavenly audience sang loud hallelujahs to his proclamation and his justice. Then the Creator, calling forth by name certain angels, gave them charge what changed elements must meet the disgraced condition of man. The sinless world had avoided pinching cold and scorching heat, and on Earth perpetual spring might have smiled equally all the days and nights. But now he bid his angels move the Sun off his perfect point of center in the orbiting planets, and push the poles of Earth beyond ten degrees twice oblique from the Sun's axle, to affect the planet with seasons of cold and heat scarcely tolerable in their extremes. Then he prescribed the planetary motions, when to join in unbenign conjunction, to shower their astrological sphere of malignant influence. These changes in the heavens, though slow, brought their counterpart on sea and land: vapor mist and hot eruptions, thunder rolling terror through the dark inner bowels of the land, and from the north, potent winds armed with ice and snow and hail to rend the woods and upturn seas. Thus began outrage from lifeless things.

Now Discord, first daughter of Sin, was introduced to the irrational creatures by Death. Beast began war with beast, fowl with fowl, and fish with fish. All left the grazing of the herb to devour each other instead. No longer in wondrous awe of man, they fled him, or with grim countenance glared on him as he passed. Adam, who hid in gloomiest shade, abandoned to sorrow, began already to see around him these growing miseries, while within him yet worse passions grew.

Was this then the end of that new glorious world and of him that now hid from the face of God? Well enough if here would end the misery. But why did he yet live, mocked with death? How gladly would he have met his sentence of mortality and be insensible to Earth—welcome hour, whenever! How gladly would he have laid himself down, as in his mother's lap, there to rest and sleep secure, that dreadful judgment no more to thunder in his ears, to torment him with fear and cruel expectation of worse to come. Yet, one doubt pursued him: what if, after all, he could not die? What if that pure breath of life with which God inspired the spirit of man could not together perish with his body of clay? Then, in the grave, or in some other dismal place, who knew but that he might die a living death, a thought too horrible to think.

The Lord of all was infinite; was his wrath also? Man was not infinite, but doomed to mortality. Then how could God exercise wrath without end on man, whom death must end? Could he make deathless death? Would he draw out, for anger's sake, finite to infinite, extending man's sentence beyond nature's law, to satisfy his never satisfied vengeance? What if death were not one stroke, depriving sense, as he supposed, but endless misery from that day onward, felt within him and without him, and so lasting to eternity? That dreadful fear came thundering back to him, that death and he would be found eternal, united in one body—nor he alone, for in him all posterity stood doomed. Such legacy must he leave his sons. If only he were able to waste it all himself and leave them none, how they would bless him who was now their curse. Why should all mankind be condemned for one man's fault? God's justice seemed inexplicable. But too late did Adam dispute those terms that should have been refused when they were proposed, having enjoyed the goods, then arguing the price. But were the wrath to fall on him alone as he wished, could he support that burden, heavier than the Earth to bear, though divided with the guilty woman? Both what he wished and feared alike destroyed all hope of refuge and rendered him miserable beyond all past or future example, likened only to Satan in crime and doom.

Into this abyss of fears and horrors he was driven by conscience, all his vain evasions and maze of reasoning only plunging him deeper and deeper. Thus Adam loudly lamented to himself through the still night, which was not wholesome and cool and mild as before man fell, but accompanied with black air, with damp and dreadful gloom, which to his plagued conscience represented all things with double terror. On the cold ground he lay outstretched and cursed his creation and death's delayed threat, overhanging since the day of his offense.

"Why does death not come," he moaned, "with one welcome stroke to end me? Shall truth fail to keep her word, or divine justice not hasten to be just?"

But Death does not come at call, and Justice does not alter her slowest pace for prayers or cries. Such cries echoed the woods and fountains and hills, whose spirits had not long ago resounded with far different song. Watching him afflicted so, Eve approached and tried to assuage his fierce passion with soft words, but harshly he repelled her advances:

"Out of my sight, serpent!" he cried. "For that name best befits you, leagued with him, yourself as false and hateful. Only in shape are you lacking, and color, to warn all creatures of your inward deceit, before that too heavenly form lures them into hellish falsehood and ensnares them.

"I trusted you from my side, imagined you wise, mature, loyal, and did not know that all was show, all but a rib, crooked by nature, bent, as now appears, more to the left side from which it was drawn. Better it should have been thrown out as superfluous. Oh, why did God, who wisely peopled highest Heaven with masculine saints, create at last this novelty on Earth, this defect of nature? Could he not find some other way to generate mankind? This mischief would not then have befallen, nor the endless mischief yet to come on Earth through female snares and entanglement with this troublesome sex."

He turned from her, but Eve, with unceasing tears and tresses all disordered, fell humble at his feet and, embracing them, implored him:

"Do not forsake me, Adam! Heaven is witness to what sincere love and reverence in my heart I bear for you. If I deceived you, it was unknowingly; if I offended you, it was unwillingly. Do not take from me your gentle looks, your help and advice in this uttermost distress. You are my only strength and stay. Without you, where can I go? How will I continue? While yet we live, though it be one short hour, let there be peace between us. We have the same enemy: the cruel serpent. Do not exercise on me your hatred for this misery befallen us both. I am already the more miserable of us two. Both have sinned, but you against God only, I against God and you. I will return to the place of judgment and there cry and plead that Heaven remove all the sentence from your head and place it on me, sole cause of all this woe."

She ended, weeping, and her lowly admission of fault and self-reproach won Adam's pity. Soon his heart relented towards her, so recently his life and sole delight, now at his feet, submissive, distressed, seeking reconcilement, his counsel and his aid. As one disarmed, he lost all his anger, and with peaceful words and gentle touch upraised her:

"Again unwary and too eager, woman, as before, you would pursue what you know not of. You would call his full wrath and punishment all down on your frail self, though hardly can you bear even my own displeasure. But if prayers could alter his high judgment, I would speed to that place before you and be louder heard that all might be visited on my head and your weaker sex forgiven. But prayer no more avails against his absolute decree than breath against the wind, blown stifling back on him that breaths it forth. So rise, let us not fight or blame each other. Our burden of blame is heavy enough. I now see this day's sentence of death will not come sudden, but a slow-paced evil. Nor will I hide what thoughts have risen in my unquiet breast of ways to relieve our misery, or devise its end, though sharp and sad.

"Miserable it is to be the cause of misery to others who must be born to certain woe. Pity for our descendants must concern us most. In our power it lies to prevent, before conception, the unblest race. You are childless; remain so. Let Death be cheated out of his feast and be forced to satisfy his ravenous hunger with us two.

"And if we find it hard to abstain from love's sweet embraces, conversing, looking, desiring, languishing in each others presence without hope, which would be misery and torment no less than of what we dread, then let us at once be free, both ourselves and our wretched unborn, from what we fear for both. Let us seek Death. And if we do not find him, let us with our own hands direct his destruction upon ourselves.

Why should we longer stand shivering under fears
that show no end but death, when we have the power
of many ways to die and can choose the shortest?"

He ended here, or vehement despair broke off the
rest. Eve's cheeks were dyed with pale, so much of
death her husband's words had weighed upon her.
Heartbroken by his misery, yet strengthened by his
forgiveness, she responded:

"Adam, your acceptance and regained love are
my sole consolation. By sad experience I know how
little weight with you my advice will henceforth
hold, but your sadness of which I am the cause has
distorted your reason. Nor reason alone, but other
influences urge me against your plan. Of late I have
sensed intimations of second life within me, stirring
hope amidst all sorrow. It may be only natural pity
for the future race I feel, but if these signs express
timely instinct awakened, then talk of abstinence
comes perhaps too late, and to end our race, instead
of two, we must murder three. Compared to this, my
death and yours seem easy to bear. But to add to
ours the death of our offspring, and be its cause, my
created mind contains no faculty or capacity. So strong
is my impulse to protect this unknown, invisible life
inside me, that all other appeals from Heaven or
Earth are superseded—even reason, were reason to
lead to death for all.

"But do not doubt that God has better armed his
vengeful ire than to be forestalled by our death self-
imposed. Such an end to life may prove no utmost
end to misery. Let us not provoke him further, but
seek some safer resolution, which I think I have in
view, calling to mind part of our sentence: that my
seed shall bruise the serpent's head. This can only

mean our grand foe, Satan, who contrived this deceit against us, through me, in the serpent's form. To crush his head would be revenge indeed, which would be lost by death brought on ourselves and our offspring, or childless days resolved as you propose. Our foe would escape his ordained punishment, while we would double ours.

"Adam, your renouncing of life and pleasure argues something in you more sublime and excellent, but to seek self-destruction refutes that excellence and implies not renouncement, but anguish and regret for loss of life and pleasure overloved. Let us have no more talk of violence or childlessness that cuts us off from hope and feeds our bitterness and resentment of God and his just domination over us."

She ceased, unable to discern from Adam's weary face whether her urgent plea had restored or oppressed his spirit all the more.

"Eve, now I see what great gift God has given me in you," he quietly said at last. "Much more than pleasant charms or mere beauty, you offer wisdom and promise beyond all expectation, to lift me out of hopelessness and turn my thoughts from sad endings to joyful beginnings. This life's burden, shared with you, becomes small, as your small burden promises great future joy—result of our mutual love. Through God's mercy, this blessing may lighten our pain."

He drew her close, resting his cheek on her brow. "Remember with what mild temper he heard and judged, without wrath or malice. When most severe he seemed, yet from him favor, grace, and mercy shone. We expected death to fall on us immediately that day. Instead, to you, only pains in childbearing were foretold, and these soon to be ended with such joy brought forth from your womb—already wakened to early signs of multiplying life. On me, the curse rebounded from the ground: with labor must I earn our bread. What harm is this? Idleness would be a worse sentence. My labor will sustain me. And so that cold or heat should not injure us, he has provided us these garments, pitying while he judged. This he gives without being asked; how much more will his ear be open to our humble prayers and his heart inclined to compassion."

But now the sky began to change its face in the mountain, and the wind blew moist and keen, shattering the graceful weeping limbs of the fair spreading trees, which seemed to bid the sorry pair seek some better shelter before cold night descend, a premonition of the inclement season to come.

"There is no better we can do," he continued, "but return to the place where he judged us, and there fall prostrate and humbly confess our faults and beg pardon. Surely he will relent from his displeasure with us and will instruct us and teach us further by what means to shun the harsh elements, and what else we may do to lessen whatever evils our own misdeeds have wrought. Then we need not fear to pass through this life, sustained by his strength and comfort, till we end in dust, our origin and destiny."

Expulsion

MIXED sighs and repenting whispers breathed from the unhappy couple now winged for Heaven with speedier flight than the loudest lamenting out-cry, evading envious winds that would divert them. Dimensionless, they passed in through heavenly doors, where man's Great Intercessor clad them with incense from the highest altar and presented them before his parent's throne:

"Receive, Father, these prayers I bring you in this golden censer. Behold the first fruits of that grace which you implanted in man, sown with contrition in his heart from your seed, fruits of more pleasing savor than those which all the trees of Paradise could have produced by his own cultivating hand before he fell from innocence. Now bend your ear to supplication; hear his silent sighs. If he be at loss to know with what words to pray, let me speak for him and be his advocate. Infuse in me all his works, that my merit may perfect those good—as for those bad my death shall pay. Accept, through me, these prayers for peace toward mankind. I plead not to reverse, but mitigate his doom, which is death. Let him live reconciled before you, that his days, though sadly numbered, shall ultimately yield him to a better life, where, redeemed, he may dwell in joy and bliss, made one with me, as I am one with you."

"Son, all your requests I accept for man," said the Father, "but the law I placed in nature forbids that he longer dwell in Paradise. The pure, immortal elements of that place can know no gross, unharmonious mixture and must eject him, now tainted, and purge him off as an infectious disease. Now he is subject to mortal food and impure air, as may best dispose him for death, that final dissolution wrought by sin, first corrupter of all things. I created him endowed with two fair gifts: happiness first; and second, to infinitely extend its bounds, immortality. The first fondly lost, the other serves only to eternalize his sorrow. So death becomes his final remedy, and after life tried in sharp tribulation and refined by faith and faithful works, he shall be awakened in the renovation of the just, to second life, and resigned up to Heaven. But let us call together all the blessed through Heaven's wide bounds. I will not hide my judgments from them, but let them know how I proceed with mankind, as late also they saw my reckoning with sinning angels, and seeing, thereby in their faith stood yet more firm."

He ended, and the high signal was given to the bright minister that watched, who blew his trumpet, heard once before when Heaven celebrated the consecration of the Holy Son; heard since when God descended as man; and which perhaps once more will echo to sound the general doom. The angelic blast filled all the regions, and from their blissful bowers of verdant shade, by the waters of life, fountain or spring, wherever they sat in fellowships of joy, the sons of light hastened forth in response to the high summons, and took their seats to hear pronounced from his supreme throne the Almighty's sovereign will:

"Sons of Heaven, like one of us, man has come to know both good and evil since his taste of that forbidden fruit, but let him boast his knowledge of good lost and evil got. Happier would he have remained had he stayed content to know good by itself and evil not at all. Now he sorrows, repents, and prays forgiveness, moved by my spirit in him. But I know how changeable and vain his heart can be, left to itself. Therefore, lest his now bolder hand reach also of the Tree of Life, and eat, and regain for him his immortality unsanctioned, I decree to remove him and send him forth from the garden, to till the ground from which he was taken.

"Michael, you I charge with this command. Take with you your choice of flaming warriors from among the cherubim, in case the fiend may raise some new trouble—as perhaps, pretending to act on man's behalf, he attempts to invade and take possession of that vacant Paradise. Haste forth and without remorse drive out the sinful pair from the Paradise of God and announce perpetual banishment to them and their children. And if patiently they obey your bidding, do not dismiss them in hopelessness, for their effusive tears will conceal much terror at the sad sentence rigorously implemented, but reveal to Adam what shall come in future days, as I shall enlighten you; and so send them forth, though sorrowing, yet in peace. And on the east side of the garden, where entrance up from Eden is easiest, place cherubic watch and a sword of flame waving wide and visible from afar to frighten off all who approach. Let it guard all passage to the Tree of Life, lest Paradise become a receptacle to foul spirits and all my trees their prey, with whose stolen fruit they once more set out to delude man."

The archangel prepared for swift descent, and with him, a bright cohort of watchful cherubim, of which each had four faces encompassed round, with ever-wakeful eyes that saw into the deepest night as day. Meanwhile, with its sacred light, dawn had reawakened the world and embalmed the Earth with fresh dew when Adam and first matron Eve ended their prayers, he with new strength added from above, she with new hope risen out of despair, yet linked with fear. These sentiments, each deigned to share with the other, Adam thus beginning:

"Eve, well we know that all the good we enjoy descends from Heaven, but hard it is to imagine that whatever we might say should ascend also to Heaven so high to concern the mind of God or incline his will. Yet so is every prayer upborne even to the seat of God, be it only one short sigh of human breath. For since I sought by prayer to appease the offended Father, and kneeling before him, humbled my heart, I felt as if I saw him, placable and mild, bending his ear. I grew persuaded that I was heard with favor, peace returned home to my breast, and I remembered his promise that your seed shall bruise our foe, which in my dismay I failed to understand. Yet now by this I am assured that the bitter threat of death is past and we shall live. Eve, you are rightly called mother of mankind, mother of all things living, since through you man is to live, and all things live for man."

With sad demeanor, Eve responded: "Unworthy am I that such should describe me, a sinner, ordained helpmate for you, who became instead your snare. To me belongs reproach and distrust and all blame. My Judge is truly infinite in pardon, that I, who first brought death on all, am graced by him and called the source of life.

"But the field calls us to labor, though our night has been sleepless. See how the morning begins her rosy progress, smiling, unconcerned with our unrest. Let us go forth together. Never again shall I stray from your side, wherever lies our day's work, however long we toil in sweat new-imposed. While here we dwell what burden can dispirit us in these pleasant walks? Here let us live, though in fallen state, yet content."

So spoke, so wished Eve in all humility, but all ignored by fate. Nature, her short blush of morn eclipsed with clouds, first gave signs impressed on bird, beast, and air. Hidden from the Sun's protective sight, the eagle swooped from his airy tower to drive before him two birds of gayest plume. From out of the wood sprang the lion, first of hunters, in downhill pursuit of a gentle deer, fairest of all the forest. Direct to the eastern gate their flight was bent. Adam pursued the chase with his eye, and whispering, to his wife conveyed his presentiment:

Paradise Lost

"Some further change nigh awaits us, Eve, which Heaven shows in these mute signs in nature, omens perhaps that we are too confident of our discharge from penalty, or to remind us we are dust, and must there soon return and be no more. What else could this double flight signify?—pursuit in the air and over ground toward one place, both in the selfsame moment while in the east darkness cuts the morning light. But see, in the west a radiant cloud draws over the dark sky and slowly descends with some heavenly cargo."

He was not mistaken, for by this blazing cloud the angelic bands alighted in Paradise upon a hill down from a somber sky, and would have proven a glorious apparition, had not doubt and carnal fear that day dimmed Adam's eye. There the commander left his powers to seize possession of the garden, while he alone took his way to find where Adam lodged.

Majesty enveloped his approach, though he came not in his celestial shape, too bright for sinful eyes, but clad as man, to meet man, not sociably mild as Raphael, but solemn and sublime. Over his bright arms flowed a military vest of purple and rainbow-dipped fabric. His starry helmet, unbuckled, showed him prime in manhood where youth ended. From a glistering belt by his side hung the sword that was Satan's dire dread, and in his hand the spear. Adam bowed low, while the hierarch inclined not from his princely posture, declaring as he came:

"Adam, Heaven's bidding needs no explanation, but suffice to say that your prayers are heard, and the sentence of death due when you did transgress has been stayed many days of grace given you in which you may repent and cover with many deeds well done that one bad act. Then may the Lord, appeased, redeem you from death's claim. But meanwhile, no longer will he permit you to dwell in Paradise, whereby I have come to remove you and send you forth from the garden, to till the ground from which you were taken."

He continued no further, for Adam stood heartstruck with chilling grip of sorrow at the news, all his senses bound. Eve, who had timidly retired, heard all and made her whereabouts known with audible lament:

"Oh unexpected stroke, worse than death! Must I leave this Paradise, my native soil, these happy walks and shades, fit home for gods? Here had I hoped to spend the rest of these quiet though sad days. Who shall tend these flowers, raised with tender touch from opening bud, my first visitation each morning and last each day? Never will they grow but in this climate, watered by these ambrosial fountains. How shall I part from this bower of my wedding, made sweet to sight and smell by my own hand? Compared to this, all other worlds are obscure and wild. How shall we breathe in other air, less pure, once accustomed to live in Paradise?"

"Do not mourn, Eve," said Michael, "but resign yourself to what you have justly lost. Do not set your heart on what is not yours. You are not alone; with you goes your husband, whom you are bound to follow. Where he abides, take that to be your native soil."

At these words, Adam recovered his scattered spirits and humbly addressed the angel:

Paradise Lost

"High prince, gently have you dispatched your wounding message, the less to wound; but what greater sorrow could be laid upon our frailty than what your tidings bring: departure from this happy place that was our only consolation left in despair. From this, all other places appear inhospitable and desolate. Where then are we exiled? Here, though deprived of his blessed countenance, I could frequent in worship each place which he favored with his divine presence. To my sons I could relate that on this mount he appeared, under this tree stood visible, among these pines his voice I heard, here by this spring I talked with him. So many altars would I raise of lustrous stones from the brook, monuments to the ages, and thereon offer sweet-smelling gums and fruits and flowers. Where in the next dark wilderness shall I seek his bright appearances, or trace his footsteps? For though I fled his anger, now would I gladly behold but a glimpse of his glorious robes."

To this, Michael kindly replied, "Not only Heaven is his, nor this hill alone, but all the Earth. His omnipresence fills land, sea, and air, and every kind that lives, aroused and warmed by his life-giving power. All Earth he gave you to possess and rule—no small gift. Do not suppose, then, that his presence is confined to these narrow bounds of Paradise or Eden. This would have been perhaps your capital seat, from which would spread all generations to all the ends of Earth, who would here return to celebrate and revere you, their great father. But you have lost this preeminence, brought down to dwell on even ground with your sons. Yet do not doubt that in those valleys and plains God is there, and many a sign of his presence will be found still following you, still encompassing you with goodness and paternal love.

"That you may be confirmed in your belief, before you depart from this place I am to show you what shall come in future days to you and to your offspring. Expect to hear of good mixed with bad, of supernatural grace contending with the sinfulness of men, and in hearing this, learn true patience and to temper joy with fear and pious sorrow, and thereby gain the strength to bear what state may come, prosperous or adverse. So shall you lead your life safest, and best be prepared to endure your mortal passage in its time. Ascend this hill with me now, and you shall see the future; let Eve sleep here, for I have drenched her eyes."

It was the highest hill of Paradise, from whose top the hemisphere of Earth lay stretched out in full prospect, wide and clear. Here it was that man and angel once sat in happier discourse, in tranquility now extinct, when Raphael visited Eden. With herbs of euphrasy and rue, Michael purged from Adam's eyes the unwholesome film caused by that false fruit which had promised clearer sight, and from the well of life, instilled three drops to augment the visual nerve. So deep the power of these ingredients pierced, even to the inmost seat of mental sight, that Adam, forced to close his eyes, sunk down and became entranced. But by the hand the gentle spirit raised him and recalled his attention:

"Adam, now open your eyes and see the effects which your original crime has wrought in some of your descendants, who never touched the prohibited tree, nor conspired with the snake, nor sinned your sin, yet from that sin inherit the weakness that brings forth more violent deeds."

He opened his eyes and saw new things: a field partly tilled with new-reaped sheaves of grain, the other part grazed by folds of sheep. In the midst stood a grassy altar. A sweaty farmer brought the first fruits of his labor: the green ear and the yellow sheaf, yet unculled and crude. A shepherd next came, more thoughtful, with the firstlings of his flock, the choicest and best. He laid the entrails and their fat, strewn with incense, on the cut wood, and performed the rites of sacrifice. His offering was soon consumed by Heaven's fire; the other's not, for it was not sincere. Whereby grew jealousy and inward rage as they talked, till with a stone one struck the other a deadly blow that beat out life. He fell, pale and bloody, and groaned out his life. At that sight Adam was much dismayed in his heart and cried to the angel:

"Teacher, some great harm has befallen that meek man who had so devoutly sacrificed! Is this the way piety and worship are paid?"

"These two are brothers," replied Michael, who was not unmoved, "the first to come of your seed. The unjust has slain the just for envy that his brother's offering found acceptance from Heaven. But the bloody deed will be avenged and the other's faith rewarded, though here you see him rolling in gore."

"Sad are both the deed and the cause," said Adam. "But have I now seen death? Is this the way I must return to native dust, this sight of terror, foul and ugly to behold?"

"You have seen death in his first shape on man," said Michael, "but death takes many shapes, and many are the ways that lead to his grim cave, all dismal, yet more terrible at the entrance than within. Some, as you saw, shall die by violent stroke, some by fire, flood, or famine, but many more by intemperance in their food and drink, which shall bring dire diseases to Earth. Of these, a monstrous mixture shall now appear before you, that you may know what misery the indulgence of Eve shall bring on men."

Immediately, before his eyes appeared a place, sad, dark, and noisy, wherein were laid all number of diseased souls, all afflicted with maladies of ghastly spasm or joint-racking torture, asthmas and qualms of heart-sick agony—all feverous kinds: convulsions, epilepsies, fierce inflammation, intestinal stone and ulcer, colic pangs, demoniac frenzy, morbid melancholy, and moon-struck madness. Dire was the tossing and deep the groans. Despair tended the sick, busied from bed to bed. And over them, triumphant Death shook his dart, but delayed his strike, though much invoked by these as their merciful hope and final cure. What heart of rock could long behold such deformed sight dry-eyed? Adam could not, but wept, though not born of woman.

"Oh miserable mankind," he cried, "degraded to such wretched state! Better to end here, unborn. Why is life given, to be wrenched from us so viciously? Can this be the divine likeness of God in man, so fallen, created once so erect and sublime, now debased to such unsightly sufferings, under inhuman pains? Should not men be free from such deformities, if only for their Maker's image sake?"

"Their Maker's image forsook them when they debased themselves and nature to serve unrestrained appetite," answered Michael; "then they took the image of that which they served: a brutish vice, reverting back to the sin of Eve. Therefore, so wretched is their punishment, disfiguring not God's likeness, but their own, as they pervert pure nature's healthful rules to loathsome sickness, since they did not revere God's image in themselves."

"Then I submit," said Adam, "and yield to justice. But is there no other way, besides these painful passages, how we may come to death?"

"There is," said Michael, "if you observe well the rule of moderation in what you partake of Earth's bounty, seeking due nourishment, not gluttonous delight. So may you live many years, till like ripe fruit, you drop into your mother's lap, or be gathered with ease, not harshly plucked, but mature for death. This is old age. But then you must outlive your youth, your strength, your beauty, which will change to withered, weak, and gray. Your senses dulled, you must forgo all taste of pleasure, and in place of the air of youth, hopeful and cheerful, in your blood will reign a melancholy damp of cold and dry to weigh your spirits down, and finally consume life's last ember."

"Then I will not shun death, nor much prolong life, but more be concerned how I may end this cumbrous burden quickest and easiest," said Adam.

"Do not hate your life, nor love it," replied Michael, "but what you live, live well—how long or short leave to Heaven. And now prepare for another sight."

He looked and saw wide territory spread before him, towns and cities with lofty gates and towers unveiling the fierce face of war. He saw giants of men wielding their arms or curbing their foaming steeds. In one place a band drove a herd of cattle and oxen from a wide meadow over the plain; another's booty was a flock of ewes and their bleating lambs. Shepherds barely fled with their lives, but called in aid, which brought bloody conflict. Where cattle once grazed, soon weapons and carcasses lay scattered over deserted green fields turned red.

Adam turned to his guide in tears: "These are Death's ministers, not men, who deal death inhumanly to men, for if they be men, then they multiply ten-thousandfold the sin of him who slew his brother, for whom may man slay who is not his brother?"

"In these days to come, only might shall be admired and called valor," said Michael. "To overcome and subdue nations in battle and bring home spoils through endless manslaughter shall be the highest of human glory, and great conquerors shall be styled of such glory and called gods and sons of gods— more rightly called destroyers and plagues of men. So will fame be achieved on Earth, and what most truly merits fame remain hidden in silence. But only the meek shall walk with God; what punishment awaits the rest, now direct your eyes and see."

Again the face of things was changed. The brazen voice of war had ceased to roar, and all was turned to merriment and games, to feast and dance, with marriage or prostitution, whichever suited, or adultery, as the whim struck, or rape. And so amusement spread from drink to bed to brawl. At length, a reverend father came among the horde and testified against their riotous ways. He preached conversion and repentance, but all in vain. When he saw the futility of his effort, he ceased and removed his tents far off, and began to lead his sons in building a vessel of huge bulk from tall timbers hewn on the mountain. In the side was cut a large door, and within, bounteous provisions laid for man and beast. Then, strange wonder, of every beast and bird and insect came pairs, and in their order entered in, followed by the father and his three sons, with their four wives.

Meanwhile the south wind rose, driven by black clouds hovering wide, as the hills exhaled up vapor to add to their supply. The thickened sky stood awhile like a dark ceiling, then down rushed the rain, not ceasing till the Earth was seen no more. The floating vessel swam, uplifted, and rode secure, tilting over the waves. All other dwellings were overwhelmed by flood, and their inhabitants, with all their debaucheries, sent down under water. Sea covered sea, sea without shore, and in the palaces where luxury once reigned, sea monsters lodged and mated. Of mankind so numerous, all that was left floated in that one lonely vessel. How Adam then did grieve!—to see the end of all his offspring. Another flood—one of tears and sorrow—sunk him down, as had the sea his sons, till, gently lifted by the angel, he stood on his feet, though without comfort, as when a father mourns his children, all destroyed in view and at once. He spoke with scarcely the strength to speak:

"Better had I lived ignorant of the future and borne my part of evil only, each day's burden enough to bear. Now the troubles of many ages light on me at once, gaining abortive birth by my foreknowledge, to torment me before their being. Let no man seek to be foretold what shall befall him or his children: evil, he may be sure, which his foreknowing cannot prevent; nor shall he feel the less its sting in apprehension than in the realization. But what man is left to warn? Those few who escape will at last be consumed in famine and anguish, wandering that watery desert. I had hoped that when violence ceased and war ended on Earth, peace would crown the race of man with long happy days; but now I see how peace corrupts, as war lays waste. How comes it to this, explain, heavenly guide, and whether here the race of man will end."

"Those which last you saw in triumph and luxurious wealth are those same first seen in acts of prowess and great exploits," said Michael, "but they are void of true virtue, and having spilt much blood and done much waste, subduing nations and achieving thereby fame in the world, shall change their course to pleasure, ease, and sloth. The conquered also, enslaved by war, shall, with their loss of freedom, lose all virtue and all fear of God, worshipping instead their lords. So all shall turn degenerate, all depraved, justice and temperance, truth and faith forgotten, one man excepted, the only son of light in a dark age, who saves himself and his household from amidst a world gone to universal ruin.

"So shall this mount of Paradise beneath us be pushed away by might of waves, inundated, all its green landscape spoiled and trees adrift, tossed and carried by the great flood to the farthest end of Earth, and there take root, an island and bare, the haunt of seals and whales, to teach how God attributes no sanctity to any place if none be brought there by men.

"Now witness, as your preternatural sight begins to fail, one last event."

Paradise Lost

Adam looked and saw the ark drifting on the flood, which abated, for the clouds were gone, driven by a keen north wind that blew dry. The clear Sun glazed hot on the wide watery glass, and drew, as if by thirst, and made the standing lake shrink and ebb with soft step towards the deep. The ark floated no more, but seemed fast fixed, as on some high mountain. A dove, twice sent forth to find a green tree where his foot might light, returned again to the ark, this time in his bill an olive leaf, sure message of peace to come. Soon the tops of hills and rocks appeared; then with furious clamor the rapid currents drove towards the retreating sea. Finally, from the ark the ancient pilgrim descended upon dry ground with all his train. With uplifted hands and devout eyes, grateful to Heaven, he beheld overhead a dewy cloud, and in the cloud a striped spectral bow, betokening peace from God and a new covenant. At this, the heart of Adam greatly rejoiced, and his joy broke forth:

"Heavenly instructor, I am revived at this last sight, assured that man, with all the creatures, shall live. Far less I grieve now for a whole world of wicked sons destroyed than I rejoice for one man found so perfect and so just that God deigns to forget his anger and raise another world from him. But say what those colored streaks in heaven mean that stretch out like the brow of God appeased. Do they perhaps serve as a flowery belt to bind the fluid contents of that watery cloud, lest it again break open and shower upon the Earth?"

"Your reason shows skilled aim," answered Michael. "So willingly does God remit his anger, though grieved at his heart when looking down he sees man so depraved, the whole Earth filled with violence and all flesh corrupt in its way; yet these once removed, such grace shall one good man find in his sight, that he relents, not to blot out mankind, and makes a covenant never to destroy the Earth again by flood, and when he brings over Earth a rain cloud, will set therein his triple-colored bow for man to look upon and call to mind his covenant. Day and night, seed-time and harvest, heat and white frost shall thence hold their safe course till this world's end."

As one who in his journey rests at noon, though bent on speed, here the archangel paused between the world destroyed and the world restored. Adam too, wearied by the cumbrance of divine sight upon mortal eyes, though elated, remained silent.

"Thus have you seen one world begin and end," resumed Michael, "and from a second Adam, new hope born. But doubt not that sin will reign again. This second source of men, while still but few in number, with the dread of past judgment recent in their minds, shall lead their lives with some regard to what is just and right, working the soil and reaping plenteous crops of corn, wine, and oil. They shall multiply and spend their peaceful days in innocent joy. Yet while still the patriarch lives who escaped the flood, men shall grow so stupid as to forsake the living God and fall to worship their own work in wood and stone for gods.

"Once again men shall rise of proud, ambitious hearts, who, not content with fraternal equality, will seize undeserved dominion over their brothers and dispossess nature's law of harmony from the Earth. Man shall style himself a mighty hunter, but men, not beasts, shall be his game. Wolves shall succeed for teachers, who turn all the sacred mysteries of Heaven to their own vile advantages of wealth and ambition. The truth shall be tainted with superstition, and false laws imposed on every conscience. So shall they presume to force the spirit of Grace itself and bind her consort, Liberty, and heavy persecution shall fall upon all who persevere in the cause of truth. Truth shall retire, bestruck with slanderous darts, and works of faith rarely be found. To good men, the world shall prove a place malignant; to the bad, benign.

"Thus will the latter, as the former world, still tend from bad to worse, till God, at last wearied with their iniquities, withdraws his presence from among men and averts his holy eyes, resolving to leave them thenceforth to their own polluted ways."

Sunk down with the weight of the future world, solemnly Adam grieved for his faulted children to be:

"Oh, what short-lived reprieve! Is man endlessly to fall?—not once, or if once, a perpetual fall through endless ages, precipitated from that first mistake that sought knowledge of good and bad, not knowing bad the longer scroll—ever-growing, it seems, of human faults heaped to the heavy sum of people's sins, shameful and accursed. Wretched man! What hope has he? Who will guide the unfaithful herd through this life's long valley of raised enemies; who them defend? Oh messenger, dreadful is the voice of God provoked to mortal ear! I pray you cease, if no more hopeful word is yours to afford. I have my fill of knowledge bad, what this mortal vessel can contain."

Expulsion

"Dear is the cost of man's first lapse from grace," answered the charitable spirit, full of solace; "nor cheaply his salvation won. Some blood more precious must be paid for man, to dissolve Satan with his perverted world and purge the masses. No mundane conqueror is equal to that victory. Hence, for man, God sends forth One Greater, whose day is foretold by all the prophets in their ages. They shall sing of the times of the great Messiah, the Holy One who dwells with mortal men. He shall quell the adversary serpent and bring back through the world's wilderness long-wandered man, safe, to an eternal Paradise of rest.

"In that day shall rise a son, the woman's seed to you foretold, foretold to kings, last of kings, for his reign shall be no end. A virgin is his mother, but his sire the power of the Most High. In him shall all nations trust. All nations of the Earth shall be blessed in that seed which is the Great Deliverer, who shall bruise the serpent's head, by which means he achieves mankind's deliverance. Then shall he ascend the hereditary throne and bound his reign with Earth's wide bounds, his glory with the heavens."

He ceased, discerning Adam surcharged with joy, as had he been weighed down in tears—this evident without vent of words, yet these he breathed:

"Oh prophet of glad tidings, you fulfill my utmost hope! Now I find my eyes truly opening and my perplexed heart much eased. Now clearly I understand that which my steadiest thoughts have searched in vain: why our great expectation should be called the seed of woman, virgin mother, hailed high in the love of Heaven; yet from my loins she shall proceed, and from her womb, the Son of God most high. So God with man unites. Then must the serpent expect his mortal bruise. Say where and when shall their fight occur; describe what stroke shall bruise the Victor's heel."

"Dream not of their fight as of a duel," said Michael, "or the physical wounds of head or heel. This is not the purpose of the joining of God in man. Not so is Satan overcome, whose fall from Heaven, an even deadlier blow, did not disable him from dealing you your death's wound. Not by destroying Satan, but his works in you and in your seed, is your deliverance won. Nor can this be, except by fulfilling the penalty of death withheld from you. Only by suffering the penalty owing to your transgression, and to theirs which out of yours will grow, can high justice rest fulfilled. And perfectly shall he fulfill the law of God, by obedience and by love, though love alone fulfills the law. Your punishment he will endure by coming in the flesh to a reproachful life and cursed death, proclaiming life to all who shall believe in his redemption. But though he dies, his spirit shall ever dwell within all men, to write upon their hearts and guide them in all truth and arm them with spiritual armor, able to resist Satan's assaults and quench his fiery darts. For it is the Savior's bodily death which cancels your doom, the death you should have died in sin. This act shall bruise the head of Satan and crush his strength, defeating Sin and Death—his two main arms—and fix far deeper in his head their stings than worldly death shall bruise the Victor's heel, or theirs whom he redeems; for them, a death-like sleep, a gentle wafting to immortal life.

Expulsion

"Then to the Heaven of Heavens shall he ascend with victory, triumphing through the air over his foes and yours, and, entering into glory, resume his seat at God's right hand, exalted high above all names in Heaven, to come forth again when this world's dissolution is ripe, with glory and power to judge both quick and dead—to judge the unfaithful dead, sending them to Hell, but to reward his faithful and receive them into bliss, whether Heaven or Earth, for then the Earth shall be all Paradise, a far happier one than this of Eden, and of far happier days."

Adam, replete with joy and wonder, exclaimed:

"Oh infinite goodness—goodness immeasurable! That all this good shall come of evil, and evil turn to good more wonderful than that by which creation first brought forth light out of darkness! I know not how to reconcile repentance of my sin with rejoice that from it much more good shall spring: to God more glory, more good will to men from God, and over wrath grace abound!

"Supremely instructed, I have my fill of knowledge beyond which was my folly to aspire. I learn that to obey is best, to walk as ever in God's presence; that great accomplishments are born of small things—by things deemed weak the worldly strong subverted, the worldly wise surpassed by the simply meek; and that suffering for truth's sake is fortitude to highest victory."

"Having learned this, you have attained the sum of wisdom," said Michael, concluding. "For none higher could you hope were you to know every star by name, or all the secrets of the deep, or all the works of God in Heaven. All the riches of this world or its

Paradise Lost

rule under one empire would be not worth as much to you. You need only add to this knowledge deeds answerable to God; add faith and virtue, patience, temperance, and add love: the soul of all the rest. Then you will not be reluctant to leave this Paradise, but shall possess a Paradise within you.

"Let us now descend this hill for the hour of our parting is come. My guards encamped yonder are preparing leave. Before them waves a flaming sword, my signal that we may no longer stay. Go waken Eve; I have calmed her with gentle dreams and composed her spirits to meek submission. When the time is fitting, share with her all you have learned of man's impending trials and great deliverance through her seed."

They both descended—Adam to the bower, where Eve, already awake, greeted him, no longer sad:

"Where you went and what you saw I know not, but God is in sleep, and dreams also reveal. Rest has lifted my sorrow and my heart's distress, and I awoke with a presage of some great good to come. But now lead on. I will not delay to follow, for to go with you is to stay in Paradise; to stay without you is to leave Paradise behind. You are all things under Heaven to me, my home and my life."

Adam gave no answer, for Michael now hastily drew near, as from the other hill in meteoric brightness the cherubim descended to their fixed station, gliding over the ground as evening mist risen from a river. High before them the sword of God blazed fierce as a comet and began to parch the temperate air with torrid heat. In either hand the archangel caught our lingering parents and led them to the eastern gate and quickly down the cliff to the plain below, then disappeared. They looked back and beheld all the eastern side of Paradise, once their happy seat, now lost, the gate thronged with fearsome faces and fiery arms, waved over by that flaming brand. Some natural tears they dropped, but wiped them soon. The world was all before them, and providence their guide. Hand in hand, with slow and wandering steps, through Eden they took their solitary way.

19692204R00121

Made in the USA
Lexington, KY
03 January 2013